MAXIMALISM AND VISUAL DELIGHT

Jeanne Leighton-Lundberg Clarke and Contemporary Genre Painting

---

Courtney R. Davis
Melissa Hempel
Rebekah Wilson Monahan

MAXIMALISM AND VISUAL DELIGHT

Jeanne Leighton-Lundberg Clarke and Contemporary Genre Painting

---

Courtney R. Davis
Melissa Hempel
Rebekah Wilson Monahan

COMMON GROUND RESEARCH NETWORKS 2019

First published in 2019
as part of the Arts in Society Book Imprint
doi: 10.18848/978-1-86335-141-6/CGP (Full Book)

BISAC Codes:
ART015110   ART / History / Contemporary (1945-)
ART065000   ART / Women Artists
ART016000   ART / Individual Artists / General

Common Ground Research Networks
2001 South First Street, Suite 202
University of Illinois Research Park
Champaign, IL
61820

Copyright © Courtney R. Davis, Melissa Hempel, and Rebekah Wilson Monahan 2019

All rights reserved. Apart from fair dealing for the purposes of study, research, criticism or review as permitted under the applicable copyright legislation, no part of this book may be reproduced by any process without written permission from the publisher.

Library of Congress Cataloging-in-Publication Data

Names: Davis, Courtney R., author. | Hempel, Melissa, author. | Monahan, Rebekah, author.
Title: Maximalism and visual delight : Jeanne Leighton-Lundberg Clarke and contemporary genre painting / Courtney R. Davis, Melissa Hempel, Rebekah Monahan.
Description: Champaign, IL : Common Ground Research Networks, 2019. | Includes bibliographical references.
Identifiers: LCCN 2018058934 (print) | LCCN 2018059587 (ebook) | ISBN 9781863351416 (pdf) | ISBN 9781863351393 (hardback : alk. paper) | ISBN 9781863351409 (pbk. : alk. paper)
Subjects: LCSH: Clarke, Jeanne Leighton-Lundberg, 1925-2014--Criticism and interpretation. | Genre painting, American--20th century.
Classification: LCC ND237.C5717 (ebook) | LCC ND237.C5717 D38 2019 (print) | DDC 759.13--dc23
LC record available at https://lccn.loc.gov/2018058934

Cover Photo Credit: Jeanne Leighton-Lundberg, *Entertaining: Favorite Ladies III*, 1991. Utah Valley University Woodbury Art Museum, Orem, Utah. *Source: Courtesy the Jeanne Leighton-Lundberg Clarke Family Trust.*

Table of Contents

Foreword ix

Chapter 1 1
Color & Pattern: A Formalist Analysis
    Shape, Pattern and Color: Modernist Connections 1
    Unresolved Equivalent: Pattern & Decoration 7
    The Maximum Statement: Leighton-Lundberg and Maximalism 10
    The Maximum Statement in a Globalist World....................................14

Chapter 2 17
Reclining Figures & Self-Representation: The Growth and Development of an Artist and Her Genres
    Patterned Lives: Formal and Symbolic Connections............................19
    Pursuit: Chasing Medium and Matriarchy...21
    Merging Histories: Female Figures 23
    Nourishment: Fulfillment and Support..26
    Legacy: Influence and Family 29

Chapter 3 31
Family Life
    A Cubist Genre Scene 32
    Pattern Theory 36
    Religious Symbolism in the "Family Life" Series................................39

Chapter 4 43
Favorite Ladies
    Appropriation and "The Question"..43
    Redressing: Fashion and Modesty 46
    The Women (and their Artists)..48

Picasso: Gender Paradox 50
Degas: Beauty and the Misogynist 51
Manet and the Absurdity of the Traditional Nude 54
No Women Artists? 56
Comparison to Contemporary Feminist Artists 56
Favorite Ladies Conclusion 59

Chapter 5 61
The Maximalist Legacy
Anything and Everything: Maximal Experience and Visual Rebellion 61
More is More: Maximalist Design and Visual Overload 64
Maximalism & Contemporary Culture 66
The Legacy Continues 70

Chapter 6 71
Conclusion

Bibliography 73

Foreword

For decades, critics and historians have applied the term maximalism to artworks that embrace decorative overload and visual excess as well as to trends that counter the reductive qualities of the minimalist aesthetic. When American artist Jeanne Leighton-Lundberg[1] (1925-2014) identified herself as a maximalist in 1980, she may have been the first artist in contemporary history to use the term to denote a formal stylistic approach. Leighton-Lundberg, whose work has been collected by a variety of museums in the western United States, painted modernist inspired contemporary genre scenes that explored womanhood and traditional gender roles at the height of Second Wave Feminism. Not unlike the spirit of Judy Chicago's iconic Dinner Party (1975-79), Leighton-Lundberg created banquet tables hosting famous women appropriated from the art historical canvases of such artists as Edgar Degas, Pablo Picasso, and Andy Warhol. Yet, despite the avant-garde nature of her work, which incorporated both maximalist and appropriative tendencies, little has been written on Leighton-Lundberg's contributions to contemporary American art. The authors seek to fill the gaps in art historical scholarship related to the interconnected histories of Maximalism, an artistic approach, and Jeanne Leighton-Lundberg, a maximalist artist.

First, the authors analyze Leighton-Lundberg's work (as well as related maximalist images) through an art historical lens, creating a structural framework in which to place maximalist trends in contemporary genre. The authors extensively studied the collection of the artist's paintings housed at the Woodbury Art Museum at Utah Valley University (Orem, Utah) held in the Jeanne Leighton-Lundberg Clarke Family Trust. This collection provided a gateway to understanding the historical relevance of Leighton-Lundberg's colorful and easily recognized style, which draws heavily from modernist precedence including Fauvism, Expressionism, Color Field painting, and Op Art, as well as postmodernist developments related to appropriation art and feminist art. By analyzing her approach in comparison with modernist methods, the authors seek to make Leighton-Lundberg's style both accessible and relevant to contemporary art criticism.

Drawing upon their backgrounds in museum leadership, collections management, and art history, the authors combine primary and secondary research to fill the gap in scholarship related to Jeanne Leighton-Lundberg and maximalist genre. The authors employ stylistic analysis as an art historical meeting point, a way of expanding both upon Leighton-Lundberg's approach as well as contemporary genre painting in general. In the connection, the first and last chapters focus most strongly on the

---

[1] Although publicly, the artist is known as Jeanne Clarke, the authors refer to her in the manuscript as Leighton-Lundberg, a name she adopted to honor some of the most important people in her life, including her grandmother. Just as she dubbed herself a Maximalist, the authors hope to bring her more recognition and attention, looking behind the canvas and beyond her name.

placement of maximalism in contemporary art history and the developing importance of this style. The authors rely on the most current information available regarding maximalist themes in order create a definitive resource on this artistic movement, which is currently being explored not just in painting and the visual arts but is also exerting a strong impact on graphic and interior design. These sections on maximalism and stylistic analysis provide a foundation for ensuing chapters related to message as well as legacy.

Second, the authors explore the content, symbolism, and interpretations of specific maximalist paintings produced by Leighton-Lundberg and related artists. These chapters required extensive research on Leighton-Lundberg's works, which was drawn largely from interviews conducted by the authors (including the artist's friends and family members), unpublished writings, and a scattering of published works. Rather than expecting familiarity with Leighton-Lundberg's works on the part of the readers, the authors explain content and symbolism of individual paintings, focusing strongly on message and theory. Imagery is an important component of these sections, contributing strongly to the explanations of content and symbolism. Although informed by theory, the authors view these sections as an opportunity to expand on dominant themes in Leighton-Lundberg's genre series, such as gender roles, femininity, domesticity, family life, spirituality, and even the concept of nourishment. The authors incorporate feminist and psychoanalytic theory, as well as identity theory in sections related to the "Favorite Ladies" series, reflecting the contemporary preference for interpreting artworks by theme or topic, rather than by style name or period.

Third, the authors draw upon biographical information related to the life and work of Jeanne Leighton-Lundberg formed through interviews, primary research, and meetings with the artist herself (before her passing in 2014). This biographical information is not only vital to unpacking the meaning of the artist's works and stylistic approach, it also underscores the fate of many female artists whose legacy has been marginalized in art history. Leighton-Lundberg, who actually refused to be categorized as a feminist, found maximalism the ideal style for expressing the multifaceted nature of women's lives.

Finally, this project connects Leighton-Lundberg's approach and maximalist tendencies with broader social and historical constructs, such as the representation and social understanding of gender. Feminist theory plays a central role in this project, particularly in relationship to the imaging of the femininity, from feminine ideals and female stereotypes to conceptions of domesticity and women's roles. Leighton-Lundberg took a revisionist approach to art history with her "Favorite Ladies" series by contemplating the possible psychology behind iconic depictions of women by historical male artists. Appropriated from the work of artists such as Vermeer, Manet, Degas, Picasso, and de Kooning, her whimsical dinner parties are transformed from the objects of male desire into psychological, emotional, and intellectual beings. The authors explore the connection between Leighton-Lundberg's depictions and the transformation of the female psyche during the 1970s, an era when the "plight of women" was just beginning to be understood. In this connection, the authors explore related themes of stereotype, misogyny, gender paradox, and the so-called "traditional" nude in western art history. Their goal is not simply to explain Leighton-Lundberg's approach to gender, but to expand the dialogue on the symbolism and use of gender during the late twentieth century. This research draws connections with feminist art history and the work of such pioneering and celebrated artists as Judy Chicago and Mary Beth Edelson.

With this project, the authors seek to fill the gaps in art historical scholarship related to the work of Jeanne Leighton-Lundberg and also the history of maximalist approaches to contemporary portraiture and genre painting. The authors draw from extensive primary research on the work and life of Leighton-Lundberg as well as secondary research on current maximalist trends in order to produce a serious contribution to scholarship related to contemporary art history and theory, one that could function as a seminal resource on the history of Maximalism.

Chapter 1

Color & Pattern: A Formalist Analysis

Bright, bold, and bursting with color-drenched patterns, the paintings of Jeanne Leighton-Lundberg shimmer like the intricate stained-glass panels of an abstract cathedral. Bedecked with animated hues and kaleidoscopic designs, her works flirt with visual overload, a befitting quality for someone who christened herself a maximalist. With an almost aggressive lack of naturalism, the highly saturated colors of her paintings are the antithesis of the abstract grey noise that often dominates contemporary gallery space. Her works demand attention with their vibrant luminosity and methodical patterns, which collide in an abstract tapestry of designs.

Yet, despite her vivid brush and dizzying forms, Leighton-Lundberg was surprisingly traditional in her approach to painting. Her subject matter drew from conventional art historical themes, such as portraits, still life paintings, and genre scenes. The majority of her works were painted with oils on canvas in dimensions of four by five feet or less, not atypical for a gallery painter. The artist asserted that she chose oils because of "their jewel-like quality, plastic manipulability, opacity and controllable drying time which allows more freedom and hindsight when one is not completely knowledgeable about one's statement." [2] Her brushwork could be described as controlled but painterly, a type of loose formality or casual meticulousness. Although far from painting alla prima, the artist humorously described her technique as "multi-coata."[3] While her shapes are clearly defined and articulated, they are also organic, rhythmic, and imprecise. In this connection, a formalist analysis of Leighton-Lundberg's still life paintings will provide a foundation for interpreting her work within the maximalist oeuvre. This chapter will explore the artist's connections with both modernist movements as well as the postmodernist approach Pattern & Decoration in order to place her work within the development of late twentieth-century art and the maximalist aesthetic.

Shape, Pattern and Color: Modernist Connections

The launch of Jeanne Leighton-Lundberg's career aligns with the return of the figural in contemporary art and the renewed interest in easel painting. After a post-minimalist hiatus, artists began to reexamine the potential of two-dimensional works beginning in the late 1970s and the early 1980s. Rising postmodernists threw off the yoke of avant-

---

[2] Jeanne Lundberg Clarke, "A Considered Proposition of Reality: A Maximum Statement" (master's thesis, Brigham Young University, 1980), 9.
[3] Ibid. at 7.

gardism and non-objectivity by referencing styles of the past and embracing figural content, a practice seen heavily in the work of neo-expressionist painters Georg Baselitz, Julian Schnabel, and Francesco Clemente, whose highly expressive works ushered in a new era in panting. Tucked away in the western state of Utah, Leighton-Lundberg was part of this rebirth. Her style represents an amalgam of the modernist past, appropriated and reformulated into a contemporary version of traditional genre and still life painting. Structure, color, surface decoration, and multisensory qualities are drawn from sources ranging from Post Impressionism to Fauvism, German Expressionism, and Op Art.

The return to painting in the late twentieth century brought with it a reexamination of early modernist approaches and techniques. Artists reclaimed abstraction by incorporating influences traceable to such innovators as Paul Cézanne, the so-called "father of modern painting." Reacting to the dematerialization of Impressionism, Cézanne resurrected form within his paintings, often advocating the reduction of content to basic shapes, such as the cone, the cube, and the sphere. While Cézanne's content remained traditional, taking the form of still lifes, portraits, and landscapes, his approach differed radically from the past, particularly in his use of bold, black outlines to define shape. This emphasis on form became a hallmark of the early modernists, whose reductive, abstracted shapes flickered between flatness and dimensionality. Posthumously, Cézanne would greatly impact the work of Henri Matisse, Pablo Picasso, and generations of early modernists.

Borrowing from this legacy, Leighton-Lundberg emphasized the structure of her compositions through clearly defined shapes and patterns. In her still life images, the artist painted vessels of mounded fruit atop layers of striped, floral, and polka-dotted tablecloths, often accented by patterned wallpaper and flooring. Her use of form strongly echoes the flattened planes and reductive shapes of both Cézanne and Matisse. Like her predecessors, Leighton-Lundberg combined three-dimensional modeling with abstracted patterns and shapes not intended to convey illusionistic space (see *Pears from the Harvest*, 1972, fig. 1). She embraced the concept of the "Fourth Dimension" by ignoring the perspectival rules of illusionism. Although, unlike Cézanne and Matisse, she demonstrated less of a penchant for outlines, instead, allowing form to be shaped by the sharp edges of the objects themselves.

Vivid color is a defining attribute of Leighton-Lundberg's paintings, as it was for the early modernists who influenced her work. The artist's bright palette, which often conveys an optimistic mood, is undeniably fauvist in its intensity. Absent from her works are the black-smeared, clashing tones of the early expressionists, who sought to convey personal, political, and social turmoil through jarring combinations of color. Instead, Leighton-Lundberg's works emphasize color for the sake of optical sensation, as is apparent in her still life paintings of the 1980s and 1990s. Many of these works, such *Pears from the Harvest* and *Family in Blue* (figs. 1, 2), focus strongly on the primary colors—red, yellow, and blue, with accents of green, which form a square color scheme (four colors evenly drawn from around the color circle). She also experimented with a tetradic, or double commentary color scheme, in which the predominant colors used in the composition form two complementary pairs.

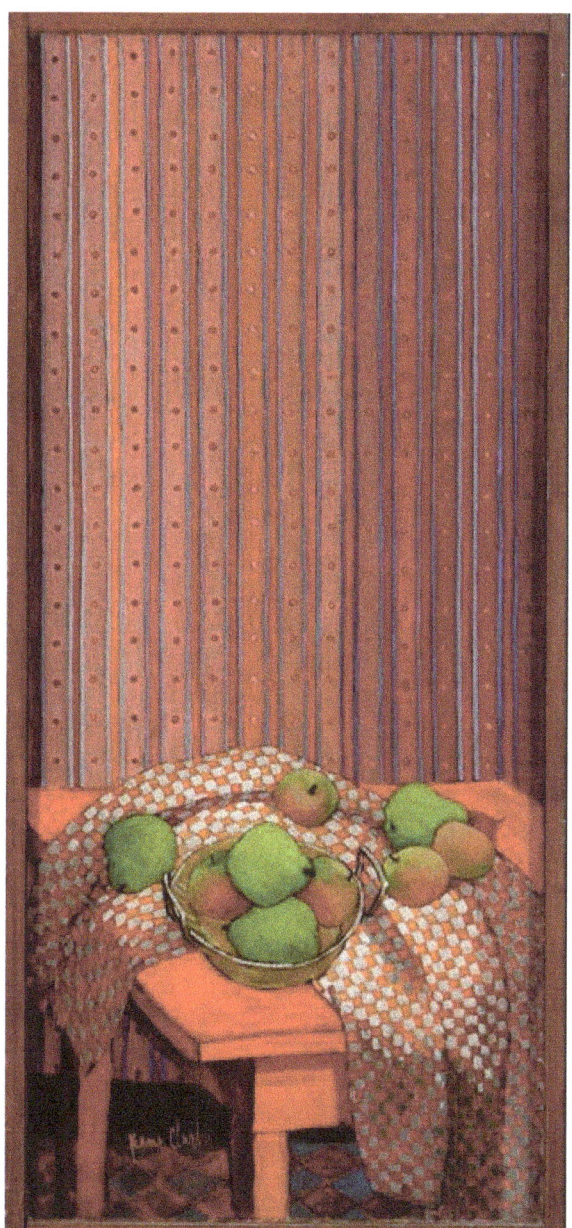

Fig. 1. Jeanne Leighton-Lundberg, *Pears from the Harvest*, 1972. Utah Valley University Woodbury Art Museum, Orem, Utah. *Source: Courtesy the Jeanne Leighton-Lundberg Clarke Family Trust.*

Maximalism and Visual Delight

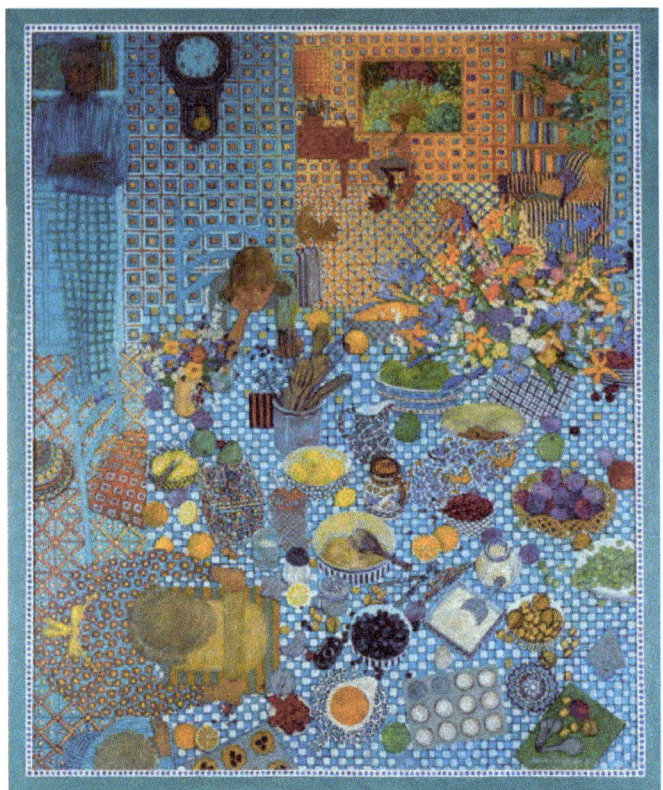

Fig. 2. Jeanne Leighton-Lundberg, *Family in Blue*, 1981.
Utah Valley University Woodbury Art Museum, Orem, Utah.
Source: Courtesy the Jeanne Leighton-Lundberg Clarke Family Trust.

Interest in the optical principles of color largely developed in the nineteenth century, particularly with the pioneering writings of French chemist Michel Eugène Chevreul (1786-1889). Chevreul, once employed as a dyest in the Gobelins tapestry factory in France, studied the principles of complementary color and developed theories explaining the phenomena of simultaneous contrast, which refers to the change in our perception of color when different hues are placed side by side.[4] Although Chevreul's theories are often discussed in relationship to the late-nineteenth-century pointilists and divisionalists like George Seurat (1859-91) and Paul Signac (1863-1935), artists of the 1960s also experimented with the principles of simultaneous contrast. These artists of the late modern era emphasized the visual potency of contrasting colors with their bold, abstract paintings of minimalistic shapes and forms, as seen with Color Field painting, hard-edged painting, and Op Art.

---

[4] This phenomenon is discussed in Chevreul's famous work, *The Principle of Harmony and Contrast of Colors* (1839).

Similarly, Leighton-Lundberg embraced the principle of simultaneous contrast in her paintings, which, as discussed above, often juxtapose vivid complementary colors, thus creating a heightened level of visual tension. Mid-twentieth-century Expressionist Hans Hofmann called this perceived tension "push and pull,"[5] arguing that our perception of colors and shapes is based upon pictorial relationships: we perceive certain combinations of forms and hues as being more dynamic than others. Warm colors seem to advance and cool colors, recede.[6] Leighton-Lundberg's vibrant paintings echo this principle, as flat surfaces transform into complex shapes and layered space.

In this connection, Leighton-Lundberg's use of color was largely inseparable from her use of form—one principle justifies and balances the other. The reductive quality of her technique draws the viewer's attention to these two artistic essentials, two building blocks that preoccupied modernists throughout the majority of the twentieth century. In his seminal treatise, On the Spiritual in Art, Russian-born German Expressionist Vasily Kandinsky devoted an entire chapter to "The Language of Form and Colour." He asserted that we have two responses when we view "a palette covered with colors," the first being pure physical enjoyment, and the second being an intellectual, spiritual, or even psychic response.[7] Form can be appreciated likewise:

> This unavoidable influence and mutual relation between form and colour causes us to observe the effect, which form has on colour. The form, even if entirely abstract and resembling a geometric figure, has its inner harmony and is a spiritual being with characteristics identical to it. A triangle (whether it is pointed, flat, or equilateral) is a decided being, possessing its very own spiritual essence. Although joined in conjunction with other forms, this essence changes and assumes novel shades, while basically it remains unaltered, as the scent of the rose, which can never be mistaken for a violet.[8]

Paralleling Kandinsky's theories, Leighton-Lundberg also utilized the dualistic nature of form and color in order to stimulate both physical and spiritual responses, particularly in relationship to visual dynamics. Kandinsky, like many early modernists, understood the perceptual connections between form, color, and movement. Noting that such ideas are based on spiritual experiences but not positive science, Kandinsky

---

[5] Hans Hofmann, Sara T. Weeks and Barlett H. Hayes, eds., *The Search for the Real and Other Essays* (MIT Press, 1967).
[6] The traditional theory that warm colors advance and cool color recede is still widely held. In contrast, Josef Albers, a prominent mid-twentieth-century color theorist, preferred the boundary theory. In his recollections of Albers' lectures, former Albers student Rob Roy Kelly asserted, "When one color butts another color, it forms a line. The line may be soft or hard according to the values. A traditional belief was that cool colors recede and warm colors advance. With the boundary theory, students discovered this was not true—it was really the boundary lines that determined spatial relationships, and not hues." Kelly, "Recollections of Josef Albers," *Design Issues* 16 (Summer, 2000), 16.
[7] Vasily Kandinsky, *On the Spiritual in Art*, ed. and trans. Hilla Rebay (New York: Solomon R. Guggenheim Foundation): 39, https://openlibrary.org/books/OL24645958M/On_the_spiritual_in_art
[8] Ibid. at 46.

asserted that yellow and blue together create a sense of movement "to and from the spectator." If a blue and yellow circle of the same size is juxtaposed, he argued, the yellow circle will appear to advance, and the blue will appear to recede "like a snail hiding in its shell."[9]

The juxtaposition of polka dots, stripes, grids, lattice, and flowers in Leighton-Lundberg's vividly hued works create an almost dizzying sense of optical motion that outstrips even Kandinsky's descriptions. In this respect, the artist herself specifically identified both kinetic art and Op Art as influences on her work.[10] While kinetic art typically incorporates movement literally, Op Art relies upon the optical suggestion of movement. Op artists often employ painstaking hard-edged lines and shapes in order to achieve the visual tension needed to create an optical illusion. Although the concept of optical illusions and tromp-l'oeil were by no means a modernist invention, the Op movement reached a pinnacle in the 1960s with artists like Victor Vasarely and Bridget Riley, whose nonrepresentational paintings of waving lines, bulging orbs, and concentric cubes appear to warp, bend, twist, swell, and even flash.

Leighton-Lundberg's works embody a similar multisensory quality: viewers' eyes skim the vibrating surface of her paintings, where patterns seem to separate from the two-dimensional support. In addition to decorative pattern, she also employed color to create optical effects, as did many artists of the 1960s Op movement. Early in her career, the artist asserted, "I am aware of, and have encouraged the optical effects of complementary color compositions. I would prefer these breathing effects to be a primary goal, but I have not yet concluded how this can be done. There are only glimmers of this phenomenon now taking place."[11] Although she openly admired the effects of Op Art, Leighton-Lundberg eschewed nonobjective abstraction. Because of her focus on still life and figural painting, her work shows similarities to the Early Modernists who prefigured Op, such as Francis Picabia (1879-1953), an artist associated with a range of avant-garde tendencies, including Cubism, Dada, and Surrealism. Picabia's *Optophone I* (c. 1921-22), for example, depicts a nude female figure in contour, silhouetted against radiating black and white concentric circles, a motif that would not seem out of place in one of Leighton-Lundberg's work.

These multisensory qualities, however, are not confined to the optical perception of space and movement. The artist's use of ripe, juicy colors fuse palette with palate in a distinctly synesthetic manner. Synesthesia, a word that stems from the Greek roots "together" and "sensation," refers to a neurological phenomenon in which two or more senses are crossed. A synesthete might taste color, see sound, or hear flavors.[12] Kandinsky discussed this phenomenon at length in his influential work, *On the Spiritual in Art*. When one first sees color, Kandinsky wrote, "the eye itself is enchanted by beauty and the multiple delight of colour. The observer is pleased. He experiences a pleasure similar to that enjoyed by an epicure in tasting a delicacy. The

---

[9] Ibid. at 61-62.
[10] Clarke, Thesis, 1.
[11] Ibid. at 8.
[12] Although this union of the senses is automatic for those with synesthesia, almost everyone can relate to the idea. We might like the taste of certain words, for example, or describe a voice as sweet, cheese as sharp, or a color as loud.

eye is stimulated as the tongue is titillated by a spicy dish. Or it is refreshed and soothed as a finger touching ice."[13] In content and form, Leighton-Lundberg's food-based paintings and table scenes invite the viewer to cross the sensations. As the viewer, we participate in the dining scenes laid out before us, tasting the bounty of summer fruits. The abundance of springtime flowers adds a fragrant dusting of scent, while the juxtaposition of patterns and forms create the sensation of movement.

Clearly, Leighton-Lundberg delighted in constructing visual feasts inspired by a wide variety of modernist sources and approaches. With postmodernist zest, she appropriated and reinterpreted, rewriting modern art history as a continuous present. While heavily grounded in Fauvism, Expressionism, and Op Art, she also drew inspiration from Post Impressionism and Color Field painting.[14] Yet, despite her obvious knowledge of twentieth-century trends, the artist was silent on the similarity of her work to contemporaneous movements, particularly Pattern & Decoration. Nevertheless, Leighton-Lundberg's work demonstrates strong visual and symbolic parallels to this decorative, pattern-based style, despite the artist's reserve on the subject.

UNRESOLVED EQUIVALENT: PATTERN & DECORATION

Although her work could easily be placed within the movement dubbed Pattern & Decoration, Leighton-Lundberg never referenced the style as an influence. P&D developed in the mid-1970s, largely as a response to Minimalism. Artists such as Mariam Schapiro, Joyce Kozloff, and Tony Robbin, demonstrated a strong interest in elevating ornamentation, surface decoration, and aesthetic beauty to fine art.[15] In many ways, P&D presented a type of visual overload, not dissimilar from the underlying principles of Op Art. Artists scoured the visual world for patterns, colors, and decorative forms to incorporate into their works. In a New York Times review for the exhibition, "Pattern & Decoration: An Ideal Vision in American Art, 1975-1985," the author wrote of P&D artists:

> They all asked the same basic question: When faced with a big, blank, obstructing Minimalist wall, too tall, wide and firmly in place to get over or around, what do you do? And they answered: You paint it in bright patterns, or hang pretty pictures on it, or drape it with spangled light-catching fabrics. The wall may eventually collapse under the accumulated decorative weight. But at least it will look great.[16]

---

[13] Kandinsky, 39.
[14] Clarke, Thesis, 6.
[15] Interestingly, they also experimented with optical illusions, such as Tony Robbin and his fascination with four-dimensional geometry.
[16] Holland Cotter, "Scaling a Minimalist Wall with Bright, Shiny Colors," *The New York Times*. January 15, 2008, http://www.nytimes.com/2008/01/15/arts/design/15patt.html

Although she did not align herself with the P&D movement, the decorations and motifs used within many of Leighton-Lundberg's paintings look extremely similar to P&D works, such as Joyce Kozloff's *Hidden Chambers* (1975-76), a painting that consists of brightly colored sections of painted floral and geometric quilt patterns. Critic Jeff Perrone described Kozloff's work with phrasing that could similarly be applied to Leighton-Lundberg: "Instead of literally using printed, embroidered cloth, clothing, quilts, etc., [the artist] paints the patterns, uniting them on the surface, but keeping their separate identities. She decontextualizes the patterns by making them decoration alone, removed from their functional base or object."[17] He also asserted that the artist "employ[ed] every surface save the ceiling, so the whole overwhelms at first in a dazzling array of color and pattern."[18]

The P&D movement developed as a response to "the reductive and increasingly sterile dictates of mainstream Minimalism and Conceptualism."[19] Yet, this reaction should not be restricted simply to the realm of formalism. Pattern & Decoration rebelled not only against formalistic principles, but also against the traditional confines of modernism, particularly in relationship to gender. Indeed, Norma Broude asserted that one of the main goals of the movement was to "liberate an area of visual expression that has long been feminized—and hence policed and artificially controlled—by our male-dominated and Eurocentric art establishment."[20] Thus, P&D sought to challenge the notions that it was "abstraction's inferior 'other'" and therefore a denigrated form of art because it had long been gendered as "female" in Western tradition.[21] P&D artists appropriated from Non-Western sources, such as Hispano-Arabic, Mexican, pre-Columbian, and Islamic art.[22] Unlike Western traditions, these cultures did not gender decorative art as female or consider it to be lacking in content as the phrase "merely decorative" implies.

In addition to liberating decorative art from polarization of gender and place, P&D artists also liberated medium by focusing on fabrics and fabric design. Textile art has been viewed historically as a third-tier, inferior form of art, not only because of the utilitarian nature of fabric, but because textiles were traditionally viewed as being in the female domain. Even when experimentation with multimedia abounded during the first half of the century, male artists still avoided using fabric in their works—papier collé, readymade objects and even garbage made their way into avant-garde art of the 1910s, but seldom fabric.[23] P&D artists broadened the spectrum of fine art materials by elevating the treatment of decorative form and pattern.

Leighton-Lundberg shared in this transformation with her strong interest in surface quality and textile-like designs, as well as with her focus on gender,

---

[17] Jeff Perrone, "Approaching the Decorative," Artforum XV (1976).
[18] Jeff Perrone, "JOYCE KOZLOFF," Artforum XVIII (1979).
[19] Norma Broude, "The Pattern and Decoration Movement," in *The Power of Feminist Art* (Abrams: 1996), 210.
[20] Ibid. at 220.
[21] Ibid. at 208, 220.
[22] Ibid. at 220.
[23] Fauve painter Henri Matisse, however, was influenced by textile designs (particularly arabesque patterns) during the first decade of the twentieth century.

particularly the celebration of womanhood. Whether she sought to neutralize gender stigma or elevate the idea of the feminine, Leighton-Lundberg's work shares much in common with the P&D artists, not just with content, but also with her visual aesthetic, as demonstrated above. Given these clear visual and symbolic parallels, the questions should again be asked: why did she not align herself with the burgeoning movement, or at least reference it in her writings?

Considering the era as well as the artist's geographic location, it is entirely possible that Leighton-Lundberg's silence on Pattern & Decoration was due to her unawareness of the style, at least in the early years of her artistic career. P&D was not a highly publicized movement in the 1970s and 1980s. Many practitioners were friends who worked in various, localized centers, particularly in California and New York City. Additionally, P&D artists focused on exploring underrepresented decorative mediums. Moving beyond just paint on canvas, they embraced textile art, needlework, tile work, ceramics, and printmaking. Emerging during the broader artistic shift from Postminimalism to Postmodernism, Pattern & Decoration was largely panned by the critics, which may have been due to the cross connections between P&D and Feminism. Scholar John Perrault asserts that almost as soon as the trends labeled "Pattern Painting" became "Pattern & Decoration," interest in the movement waned: "the lights were turned off. The artists kept working, but the collector-fueled, dealer-driven spotlight moved on to another."[24] Indeed, the first comprehensive survey of P&D did not even occur until 2007, when the Hudson River Museum opened the aforementioned exhibit, "Pattern and Decoration: An Ideal Vision in American Art, 1975-1985." In a review of the exhibition, Holland Cotter explained that this movement functioned "as an alternative in American art, in contrast to the painterly abstraction championed by critics such as Clement Greenberg. The energetic work of its artists challenged the status quo of Minimalism, Formalism, and Conceptualism."[25] Further, these artists "valued the bold pattern, craft, and ornament that was prompted in the 1960s and 70s by a new regard for the Women's Movement and women's esthetic drive, non-western art."[26]

As stated above it is plausible that, at least during the 1970s and 1980s, Utah-based Leighton-Lundberg was unaware of the Pattern & Decoration movement and that she cultivated her interest in pattern and decoration independently. Other twentieth-century movements and tendencies emerged similarly, with disconnected pockets of artists responding similarly—but independently—to prevailing styles. In an era when minimalist and reductivist tendencies had largely boxed artists into a conceptual corner, the desire to explore new visual and inspirational territory was being felt by artists throughout the 1970s at large, a decade of marked pluralism. In this connection, Leighton-Lundberg employed the same tools as P&D artists in a similar effort to emerge from the white walls and empty cubes of the minimalist era.

---

[24] John Perreault, "Deluxe Redux: Legacies of the Pattern and Decoration Movement," from *Pattern and Decoration: And Ideal Vision in American Art, 1975-1985*, ed. Anne Swartz (Hudson River Museum: 2007), 53.
[25] Cotter, "Scaling a Minimalist Wall."
[26] Ibid.

Yet, if she was in fact aware of the development of P&D, at least during the formative years of her career, it would not be the first time a twentieth-century artist was ambivalent about influences and connections to contemporary styles. Marcel Duchamp, for example, vehemently denied being exposed to Futurism before creating his mechanomorphic paintings of the 1910s, wherein human figures are reduced to fragmented, mechanical, almost robotic forms. Similarly, Kazimir Malevich often predated his work by several years, obviously aware of the avant-garde qualities of his suprematist compositions, also dating to the 1910s.

However, it is not necessary to trace a direct casual connection to Pattern & Decoration in order to support the theory that these parallel qualities acted as the gateway to Leighton-Lundberg's signature style: Maximalism. By incorporating vivid colors with decorative patterns and scavenged embellishments, the artist created strongly visual paintings, as demonstrated above. Yet, her practice of a maximalist approach expanded beyond mere surface qualities to the deeper levels of content and message, particularly in relationship to gender, family, and spirituality.

THE MAXIMUM STATEMENT: LEIGHTON-LUNDBERG AND MAXIMALISM

Given her diverse artistic heritage, nontraditional stage of life while pursuing her master's degree, and wealth of modernist influences, it seems only appropriate that Leighton-Lundberg would proclaim herself to be a Maximalist, which she did in her 1980 master's thesis, "A Considered Proposition of Reality: The Maximum Statement." Although Maximalism was not a widely recognized style of the twentieth century, the term has been used loosely to describe various reactions against the minimalist approaches of the 1960s and 1970s. Indeed, the word maximalism alone conjures mental pictures of layered visual images and symbolic content, intricate and voluminous details, and potential perceptual overload. In order to understand Leighton-Lundberg's use of the term as well as the historical significance of her work, it is necessary to first consider maximalist trends in the recent decades. Following a discussion of Maximalism in contemporary art, the authors will present an argument placing the artist's work in a slightly different (and new) category of painting: Maximalist P&D.

Maximalism in Contemporary Art

Although still relatively obscure, the term maximalism has gained more currency in the twenty-first century. Yet, it is more likely to be bandied in an art blog than legitimized in a critical review or treatise. In the 1980s, the term "Maximalism" seemed to be poised to enter the accepted art historical lexicon, particularly in critical discussions of the new Avant-Garde. In his 1987 book Postminimalism into Maximalism, art critic Robert Pincus-Witten used the term to refer to a range of loosely expressionistic painters, such as David Salle, Gary Stephan, and Lucio Pozzi. In his forward, Pincus-Witten explained that, "By the term Maximalism [in his previous writings] I intended to describe the pluralist tendencies that followed hard upon Postminimalism, when the often puritanical sense of discretion that marked Abstract Formalism, Minimalism and Conceptualism gave way to an unrepentant

Expressionist volubility."[27] Addressing the work of David Salle and Julian Schnabel in a 1982 article, Pincus-Witten asserted that, "the Maximalist New Wavers Down at The Clubs are all inventing art out of the conventions of middle-class popular culture."[28]

Despite this earlier treatise, artist and filmmaker Daryush Shokof claims to have been the first to apply the term to the visual arts in 1990. The Iranian-born American-educated artist, now based in Germany, issued his "Maximalist Manifesto" in 1991, which, unfortunately, does not usefully elucidate the underpinnings of the approach. Although hard copies of the manifesto are elusive, Shokof's website provides a summary:

> The movement of maximalism in reference to the arts was founded by the artist and filmmaker Daryush Shokof in 1990 in Cologne, Germany. Maximalism vis-a-vis the arts is a new way of creating art. Many common elements are shared in the art works by artists who participate in the maximalist movement. The movement was initiated by Daryush Shokof as he wrote in his one-man show catalog of paintings at Galleria Verlato in Milano, Italy in 1990; "Unbalancing the chaos = Balance = Life = Maximalism." Shokof wrote a lengthy manifesto with the title Maximalism. It was published in different catalogues of his one-man shows, as well as the maximalists' group shows in Europe and in the US from 1990 to 1993.[29]

Over the past three decades, the Maximalism tag has been used sporadically and loosely, also being applied to literature, film, and music. For example, Michel Delville tackled the concept of maximalism and music in his book, Frank Zappa, *Captain Beefheart and the Secret History of Maximalism*, published in 2005. In his review of the book, Martin Knakkergaard asserted, "Maximalism is presented as a specific genre or existential modality more or less defined by its limitlessness: anything can be seen as or turned into an expressive means of the artist, and the boundaries between what belongs to the aesthetics and what does not are fluctuating, if they exist at all."[30]

But yet, in recent years, Maximalism in the visual arts seems to have receded from the limitless scope of "anything and everything." Currently, one of the most comprehensive discussions of Maximalism was produced by the Florida State University's Museum of Fine Arts in 2007, as a catalogue to accompany a five-week exhibition, "More is More: Maximalist Tendencies in Recent American Painting." Acknowledging that Maximalism is difficult to define, the authors define the trend as a twenty-first century style, typified by artworks that are usually dense in

---

[27] Robert Pincus-Witten, *Postminimalism into Maximalism: American Art, 1966-1986* (UMI Research Press, 1987), 6.
[28] Ibid. at 291.
[29] "Maximalism," sensAgent, accessed June 8, 2015, http://dictionary.sensagent.com/Maximalism/en-en/
[30] Martin Knakkergaard, Review of *Frank Zappa, Captain Beefheart and the Secret History of Maximalism* by Michel Delville; Andrew Norris. In *Popular Music* 27, No. 2 (May 2008): 328. Stable URL: http://www.jstor.org/stable/40212389

composition, emphasize technique, address social issues, and create a sense of complexity.[31] Generally, maximalist compositions tend to embody the concept of horror vacui (from Latin "fear of empty space"), a stylistic element in which the entire surface of an artwork is filled with detail, as seen in many ancient and medieval artistic styles, such as the Greek Geometric period (900-700 BCE) and the Hiberno-Saxon era (600 to 900 AD). For a contemporary example, the work of Fred Tomaselli (b. 1956) exemplifies the maximalist interest in total compositional engagement. Tomaselli's layered collages combine cutout images with actual objects, ranging from plants, flowers, and even prescription pills.[32] His *Untitled (Expulsion)* of 2000, for example, combines leaves, pills, and insects with acrylic paint, photocollage, and resin on a seven by ten-foot wood panel. This postmodernist depiction of the biblical expulsion from the Garden of Eden features a psychedelic starburst above a recreation of Masaccio's Adam and Eve (1426-27) whose figures have been reduced to the human circulatory system. According to the artist, Tomaselli's works are meant to create windows into a surreal, hallucinatory universe.[33] He asserts that his ultimate aim is "to seduce and transport the viewer in to space of these pictures while simultaneously revealing the mechanics of that seduction."[34] This seductive quality of technique and content is a driving force for many contemporary maximalist works.

To quote contemporary maximalist painter Lilian Garcia Roig: "Though Maximalist painting is hard to explain, it is easily recognized when it is seen, a primary goal of the style. Maximalist painting has many layers, verging on visual overload in the form of narrative or technique."[35] Additionally, Roig asserts, "Maximalist painting creates an environment in which the viewer may lose him or herself. Maximalist painting is a unique style that analyzes itself without the help of critical scrutiny."[36] Perhaps this is why the trend has largely evaded critical treatises and dissections by art historians and critics.

Leighton-Lundberg: Maximalist Pattern & Decoration

When she proclaimed herself to be a Maximalist in 1980, Jeanne Leighton-Lundberg may have been the first to apply the term to the visual arts, predating both art critic Robert Pincus-Witten and artist/filmmaker Daryush Shokof by several years. As demonstrated above, Maximalism is a wily term to define, having thus far escaped formal canonization by art historians and critics. But even though Leighton-Lundberg was one of the first to apply the term, her work does not necessarily reflect the qualities of many artists who classify themselves as maximalists today. Her approach

---

[31] Tatiana Flores and Florida State University Museum of Fine Arts, "More is More: Maximalist Tendencies in Recent American Painting." (Tallahassee, Fla: Florida State University, Museum of Fine Arts, College of Visual Arts, Theatre and Dance, 2007), 3-4. http://mofa.cvatd.fsu.edu/resources/archive/pages/learning/resources/moreismore.pdf
[32] Brooklyn Museum, "Exhibitions: Fred Tomaselli," accessed June 8, 2015, http://www.brooklynmuseum.org/exhibitions/fred_tomaselli/
[33] White Cube, "Fred Tomaselli," accessed June 8, 2015, http://whitecube.com/artists/fred_tomaselli/
[34] Ibid.
[35] Flores and FSUMFA at 4.
[36] Ibid.

was less focused on exploring medium and technique, and more concentrated on an almost pop-art level of visual overload replete with color, pattern and decorative form captured in traditional oil on canvas. In this connection, her true style might best be described as a variation of Maximalism, one connected to the precepts of Pattern & Decoration.

In connection to her interest in expressing the multifaceted dimensions and complexities of women's lives,[37] Leighton-Lundberg asserted that, "Minimalist art, or non-representational art consisting chiefly of geometric shapes and forms, certainly cannot symbolize a woman's experience."[38] In her mind, Minimalism was devoid of "an associative humanistic content" and therefore "too self-centered" and "too free of obligation"[39] to do so. Maximalism, on the other hand, exudes richness, excess, heavy technical layering, dense composition, and visually stimulating content. In the artist's words:

> A painting should draw from all art knowledge for its mode and be selective of those elements which are most meaningful to the artist's expression. It should have emotional content, evoke visions, edify, and possibly serve as a decorative element—a "maximum" personification of art theory, life perspective and subjective license. It should be uniquely individual, an intuitive expression of paint, full of the sonorous materiality of the medium, yet speak from the heart with expository reverberations of tradition—salutary reminiscences of the simple and familial.[40]

In order to convey these maximalist ideas, Leighton-Lundberg employed a visual vocabulary similar to Pattern & Decoration, creating a type of Maximalist-P&D fusion; her style is neither one nor the other, but both. The artist once explained that viewers should consider the "fullest aesthetic implications" of decoration; she asked, "Would the Sistine Chapel [have been] as inspiring with a [simpler] stone ribbed vault?"[41] In her view, the Sistine Chapel is a particularly poignant because of—not in spite of—the elaborate decorations and patterns that cover the walls, floor, and ceiling. She wanted pattern to be recognized for its emotional, symbolic, and maximalizing capabilities.

In an era when representational painting was just reemerging from a decade of suppression, Leighton-Lundberg reintroduced fauvist playfulness, confetti colors, and overloaded decoration in a personalized maximalist and multisensory variation of

---

[37] Juggling various combinations of motherhood, careers, relationships, and housework, the infinitely variable experiences of women have one thing in common: complexity. Of her own life she said, "I don't have a secretary, for example, or a full-time cook or housekeeper. I have a half-acre and take care of it all myself. You name it, I've done it." Patricia Saleh, "A Feminist-Symbolist," *Fine Art Collector International* Vol. 2 No. 2 (1992): 29.
[38] Springville Museum of Art, "Clarke, Jeanne Leighton-Lundberg," accessed on June 8, 2015, http://www.springvilleartmuseum.org/collections/browse.html?x=artist&artist_id=431
[39] Clarke, Thesis, 8. Clarke used these phrases not in relationship to Minimalism per se, but in connection with color "unaccompanied by human content."
[40] Ibid. at 5.
[41] Thesis page vii, Author's Explanatory Note.

Pattern & Decoration. In this fusion of modernism and postmodernism lies her artistic legacy and contribution to the art historical canon. In the words of Jeanne Leighton-Lundberg, "A painting that speaks about life should be a fecund visual feast with meanings for all—including in its influence those who are less familiar with the visual arts as well as those educations perceptions—for life is full of range and perhaps painting can be also."[42]

THE MAXIMUM STATEMENT IN A GLOBALIST WORLD

The artist's graduate thesis further clarifies how Leighton-Lundberg's work corresponded with the range of painting from the 1970s onward. As mentioned above, other artists and historians worked to advance scholarship on Post-Minimalism, classifying and fitting together new bodies of work. Grouping such pieces comes with study and perspective, but to those creating in real-time, the art coming right before and immediately after can be inescapable. Leighton-Lundberg's proclaimed "Maximum Statement" may fall into that reactive category, but the artist more than likely named her thesis without knowing maximalism was knocking at the canon's door.

Her thesis statement is direct and concise, balancing the push and pull of reaction and inspiration. Leighton-Lundberg truly did have a story to tell. Her life existed outside of the mainstream paths taking place in the American mid-century and the decades immediately following, and she did not separate those experiences from her visual narratives. Like many artists, Leighton-Lundberg reconstructed her personal life in art, and a large portion of works draw from disconnections she felt from paintings and people. The abstract of "A Considered Proposition of Reality: The Maximum Statement" reads, "Their inspiration has come from a desire to somehow synthesize the avant-garde tendency for an over-simplified, severely abstract, two-dimensional, non-figurative color-field work and restatement of the more traditional genre painting element." [43] This summary warns readers more about what she was working against than what she was working toward. However, this stance is fertile for inspired work, and it is almost an unrequited love letter to the minimalist movement.

The artist repeatedly shared how minimalist work could never represent a woman's experience, strengthening the comparison to a dysfunctional or unhealthy relationship. The differing styles need one another to define their "better half." It also relates to Leighton-Lundberg's strong answer to Minimalism. She throws another dig at the movement in her thesis, explaining that, "Color, unaccompanied by an associative humanistic content, is perhaps too self-centered, too free of obligation-shrugging off art's opportunity to fantasize and enlighten." [44] Minimalistic qualities are all things stereotypically male: stoic, egotistical, and unattached.

---

[42] Ibid. at 5.
[43] Jeanne Lundberg Clarke, "A Considered Proposition of Reality: The Maximum Statement" (Master of Fine Arts Thesis, Brigham Young University, 1980), V.
[44] Clarke, "A Considered Proposition of Reality: The Maximum Statement," 4.

Her reaction was to provide the proverbial whole picture for her viewers. Leighton-Lundberg wanted her pieces to be more involved than others that might hang on a family's wall, so in a sense, she was elaborating for everyone. But considering her understanding and proclamation of maximalism, her styles and symbols were more targeted. Leighton-Lundberg was instructing those illiterate to familial obligations, those she probably felt would create Minimalist works.

And even just before she completed her MFA degree, in the decade preceding Leighton-Lundberg's final style, certain painters realized shape and depth as means to alter traditional canvases' minimal rectangle. Many felt this built extension allowed the piece to spread into real space.[45] Leighton-Lundberg's hopes to do this through symbolism and pattern were similar but carried more moral value than physical innovation. Her patterns dominate the canvas and garner maximum visual impact; shapes built one on top of another. In the 1960s, artists like Frank Stella and Neil Williams explored shape. Williams, for example, "allowed the edges of his image, a pattern of repeated parallelograms, to determine the painting's shape, which was appropriated zig zagged or sawtoothed." [46] The works chronologically predate Leighton-Lundberg's paintings, but can almost be thought of as a physical detail of her large-scale pieces. Frank Stella also referred to his body of shaped paintings as "maximalist paintings." [47] His venture into maximalism employs dimension with frantic borders and a strong weight, and the pieces feel more organic than Leighton-Lundberg's carefully painted scenes. His paintings may not even require careful visual inspection to understand their maximalist categorization. This series was seen as a departure and an entirely different evolved style. A timely publication from 1981 elaborates:

> There is a recent instance of such a stylistic shift, and its reception, that exemplifies this art historical view of painting. The shift occurs in the late 1970s in the work of Frank Stella. Although it could be said that this shift was presaged in every other earlier stylistic change in Stella's work after the black paintings of 1959, Stella's move to flamboyantly idiosyncratic constructed works of the past several years is by comparison a kind of quantum leap, and as such it has been taken as sanction for much of that recent painting which declares its individualism through the most ostentatious eccentricities of shape, color, material, and image.[48]

Stella was reacting to his own work and found his own way of classifying the new pieces and assigning a stylistic term. As a qualitative term, maximalism has been used to describe facets of contemporary work in China. In perhaps one of the more recent markers, a 2003 show at the University at Buffalo called "Chinese Maximalism"

---

[45] Frances Colpitt, "The Shape of Painting in the 1960s," Art Journal 50, no. 1 (1991): 52. doi:10.2307/777086.
[46] Colpitt, "The Shape of Painting in the 1960s," 55.
[47] "Frank Stella," Guggenheim Collection Online, accessed December 12, 2017, https://www.guggenheim.org/artwork/artist/frank-stella
[48] Douglas Crimp, "The End of Painting," *Art World Follies*, Vol. 16 (Spring 1981): 81.

again devised the title. Curator Gao Minglu named artists including Cao Kai, Ding Yi, and Gu Dexin as maximalist practitioners. The exhibition incorporated multiple disciplines and explained how the process of maximalist art from China is a spiritual experience, leaving the final piece as a record of the artist's deep practice.[49] Leading up to this relatively recent display, maximalist ideas were building in the previous decades, similar to the style's outlined growth in the United States. In China, "as a mentality and methodology it has developed since the '85 Movement. The process, labor-intensive and repetitious, involves both personal meditation and social critique in both the Chinese and global context." [50] Depending on authorship, the resulting pieces might be sparse or minimal and not look very busy but are essentially very full.

Imagining Leighton-Lundberg hard at work in her studio conjures the same contemplative creation process. The conceptual power of her work may be somewhat lost without her thesis as a key to navigate her maximalist typography, but the visual dominance of her picture plane means her work can be assessed in the style without conceptual support. Each overwhelming pattern imbued with moral beliefs and life lessons, allowing the artist to practice her spirituality. In this way, Leighton-Lundberg's work closely matches the tenants of the identified Chinese maximalist style. A great deal of her meditation centered on critiquing Minimalism and developing an opposing signature. Her reactive tactics relate to Stella's progressive styles and the canonical shifts during the 1960s and 1970s. Though not an official art movement, and often considered more of a means to qualify singular artists or pieces, when the quantitative realities of those individuals are looked at as a whole, the style might merit a movement.

---

[49] Kristin E.M. Riemer, "Chinese Maximalism debuts," *UB Reporter*, October 9, 2003, http://www.buffalo.edu/ubreporter/archive/vol35/vol35n7/articles/ChineseMaximalism.html.
[50] Minglu Gao, Total Modernity and the Avant-Garde in Twentieth-Century Chinese Art (Cambridge: MIT Press, 2011), 311.

CHAPTER 2

Reclining Figures & Self-Representation: The Growth and Development of an Artist and Her Genres

Depicting portraits of floral clad women basking in bountiful environments, the "Reclining Figures" series was painted between 1977 and 1991. The settings feature Leighton-Lundberg's signature patterned backgrounds filled with vivid color, references to nature, and traditions of home life. The artist's "Reclining Figures" celebrate womanhood and act as portraits, linking the series to other significant works. Examining how the images fit into historical types and Leighton-Lundberg's artistic lineage makes the "Reclining Figures" series one of her more meaningful and successful endeavors, as well as a telling marker of her personal views. After adding up the trials and successes of Leighton-Lundberg's life, her "Reclining Figures" emerge as the sum of intricate parts. Her women translate as ideal, feminine beings that the artist may have hoped to embody, yet sometimes felt confined within. They are self-reflexive expressions of worship, nourishment, and legacy, and ultimately, these layered and complex images unfold before the viewer. Always, the woman is modestly dressed and stares directly at the spectator from her reclined position. The restful poses she places them in resemble those of famous predecessors found throughout art history, creating dynamic scenes, distinctively painted in oil.

Betty Jo and Anne Davis, 1977 (fig. 3) is perhaps the initial inspiration for the "Reclining Figures" series, though more controlled in style by its commission. Two women, a mother and daughter, look out of the canvas while sitting cradled in the arms of a pink couch. The iconic flowered dress, here worn by the mother, would prove to grow busier over time. But its origins are explicit: a green fabric base growing with large blooms. The wearer's right arm is draped over her daughter's shoulder, a bouquet placed behind them, and her left hand sits on her knee. Above all the pose is relaxed and directed out of frame, which is informal and relatable. In the decade to follow, the reclining figure holds Leighton-Lundberg's attention and develops into one of her main genres. All of the same markers remain, including the background bouquet, which, in the latter half of the series, is now brought up to the forefront and exaggerated in size and composition. Her new figure is solitary, arm still draped, but over pillows, and the other hand sometimes clasping an orb.

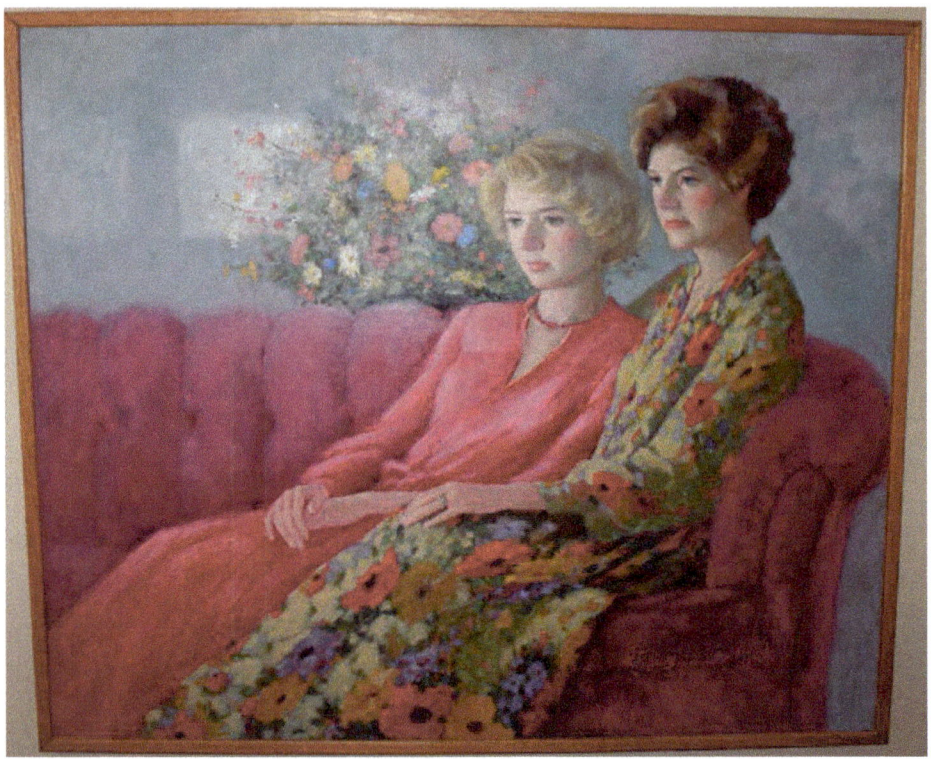

Fig. 3. Jeanne Leighton-Lundberg, *Betty Jo and Anne Davis*, 1977.
Source: Private Collection (Davis Family).

Historically, the orb is a highly symbolic addition to the paintings and interestingly connects Leighton-Lundberg's practice to traditional portraiture (a category that she found was not her calling). Earlier images of royals through the past have employed the orb as an illustration of rule and power. Since the sixteenth century, these portraits were created by court painters and followed a sometimes-formulaic pattern, placing items like orbs and scepters around the regal subject. [51] Similarly, Leighton-Lundberg's placement of bouquets, fruits, textiles, and books reflect the breadth of her figure's full life and potential rule as matriarch. Her "Reclining Figures" formula likens the women to historic kings and queens, though in a uniquely nurturing sense rather than in a display of stately power.

In the "Reclining Figures" series, the orbs represent the world, clutched by these female figures in their hands. Symbolically, the item also refers to the strength of the family unit, once again placing women in a family context, as Leighton-Lundberg often does.[52] Like a shadow, familial cares and worries are ever-present and reflected

---

[51] "Regalia," Oxford Art Online, accessed April 25, 2015, http://www.oxfordartonline.com/subscriber/article/grove/art/T071111#T071115
[52] Jeanne Leighton-Lundberg Clarke, "Inheritance 1" (Artists Statement, 1991).

in a matriarch's world, which is deeply connected to her artistic point of view. The mother is the head of the family and she never lets the orb out of her sight; it becomes entwined with her being. This meaning is made even more real in that we can identify some of the portrayed women, such as Rebecca Marriott and Leighton-Lundberg's dear friend Sharon Gray.

PATTERNED LIVES: FORMAL AND SYMBOLIC CONNECTIONS

Mostly, the "Reclining Figures" series is about pattern. This overwhelming visual element and expertly crafted quality defines the scenes. Where her "Family Life" paintings might be recognized by their individualized hues, the "Reclining Figures" dominate with multicolored pattern on every surface. The walls, tables, cushions, and clothing are all cloaked in pattern. Leighton-Lundberg's technique is most apparent in the way she weaves these colorful portions of the images together. For the artist, pattern carried great meaning:

> The pattern is representative of all of life both physical and spiritual, everything after its own kind, each leaf after its own plant, each child after his/her parents, genetically and traditionally. Patterns are taught by others, or we can create our own Holidays, months, days, numbers, earths, clouds all things are patterned. We can choose many of our patterns. Some we are locked into, but even those can be redefined according to our perceptions and attitudes.[53]

What might blend in compositionally, actually stands out symbolically to Leighton-Lundberg. She chose to cover nearly everything to convey her deep appreciation and understanding of patterns. Visually, the few objects not woven into the patterned background are the fruit of the table-scape, the subject's face, and in one, a small white cat.

In *Katherine*, the subject sits with this small white cat to her left (fig. 4). Formally, Katherine shares the same composition as the rest of Leighton-Lundberg's reclining ladies. She is the subject of a busy scene, tied together by following patterns one into another. The walls come alive with kinetic, circular designs, and the cushions support her with striped and diamonded repetitions. And of course, her beautiful green dress covered in yellow flowers matches her to Leighton-Lundberg's other female figures. Clues to her life beyond the painting include stacked books and an opening to another room. Yet, Katherine has more to reveal than figurative qualities of life, she represents Leighton-Lundberg's actual family and reflects the artist's well-remembered personality. While her daughter was pregnant with her granddaughter, Leighton-Lundberg decided to paint what she thought the future Katherine would grow up to look like. This interesting endeavor proved quite successful, as the portrait closely accounts for its current namesake.

---

[53] Jeanne Leighton-Lundberg, "Symbolist" (Artists Statement).

Maximalism and Visual Delight

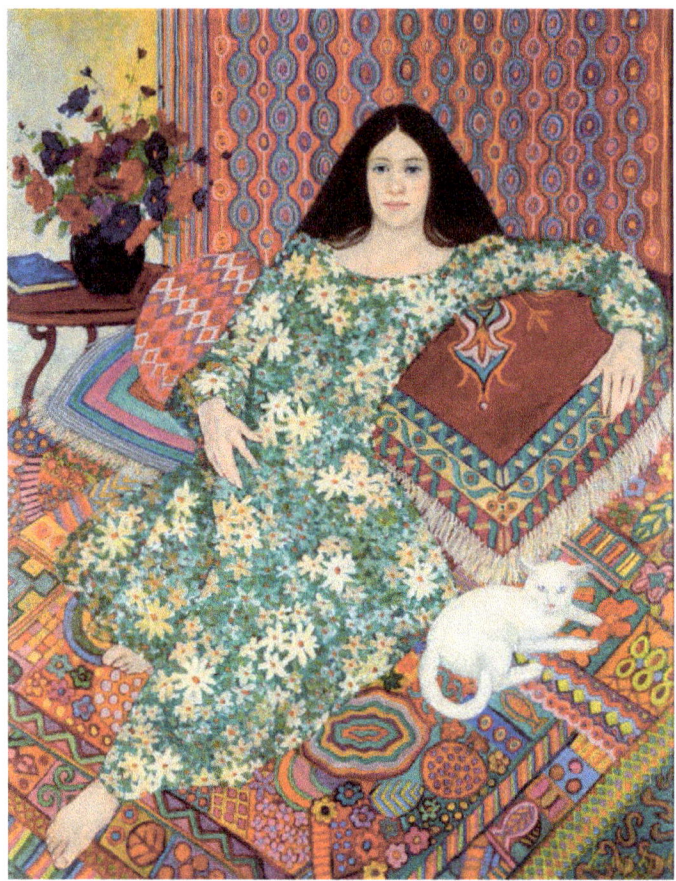

Fig. 4. Jeanne Leighton-Lundberg, *Katherine*, 1977.
Utah Valley University Woodbury Art Museum, Orem, Utah.
Source: Courtesy the Jeanne Leighton-Lundberg Clarke Family Trust.

As seen, Leighton-Lundberg's paintings provide many clues to the lives of the women depicted, whether commissioned portraits or fictional female archetypes. She paints their story, not just their likeness. Her figures' position amongst symbols of natural richness is strengthened by their somewhat idealized representations. Sharing in the representations, Leighton-Lundberg may also appear in her paintings though her presence in the "Reclining Figures" and "Family Life" series is speculated. While included, presumably she is not the subject of the works. She is generally serving the table or appearing in the periphery of the scenes. How she treats herself in the paintings is telling. No matter what type of artist or the subject matter portrayed, Leighton-Lundberg felt that all artists paint from themselves.[54] Illustrating where she subconsciously stands relates to how she felt about her talents. Leighton-Lundberg

---

[54] Patricia Saleh, "A Feminist-Symbolist," Fine Art Collector International 2, no 2 (1992): 29.

relatedly felt her place in a long line of ancestors, dedicating her master's thesis to those who passed on their "stamina" and "perseverance." She could see herself as part of a larger story.

The larger story for Leighton-Lundberg was less idealized and brightly hued than her paintings. Born in 1925 in Alpena, Michigan, Jeanne Florence Lundberg grew up in Ohio with her older sister Mary and eventually settled with her family in Chicago. Leighton-Lundberg was also born during an interesting period of American history: "The world in which blond, curly haired, blue eyed, [Jeanne Florence Lundberg] was born, was one of intellectual and cultural change, following the more conservative Victorian Age. A product of the Depression and World War II, the years of Leighton-Lundberg's youth were somewhat bleak in the history of America and of the world."[55]

It was perhaps this bleak period that young Jeanne sought to transform with her art. From that early age, she sought out an artistic outlet, and developed a deep connection to creating. Even if she was not able to formally cultivate her interests until much later in life, Leighton-Lundberg was at least secondarily exposed to various arts in the household. Her mother played music regularly and her father was a creative businessman and inventor.

PURSUIT: CHASING MEDIUM AND MATRIARCHY

As she completed high school, unlike many women at the time, Leighton-Lundberg began to think about higher education and attended the University of Chicago and the Chicago Art Institute. But she was not prepared for the rigors of study and did not complete a degree from either institution. Instead, Leighton-Lundberg would establish her own family in Westport, Connecticut after marrying for the second time at age 22 in 1948.[56] Her life's timeline mirrored the country's idea of mid-century suburban life. The "cookie-cutter" houses featured in prefabricated communities hinted at the conformity and expectations of a woman's perceived role.

As a young mother, Leighton-Lundberg raised her children, worked and began incorporating the arts into her family life, a theme that would become incredibly significant in her signature work. Leighton-Lundberg had three children, Karen, Susan, and Matthew from 1949-1955. Some of her earliest artworks were portraits of those she knew. Well-received paintings of her children, family, and neighbors in the 1950s led to paid commissions, and increased self-confidence in her artistic abilities.[57]

One of her first paid commissions in the 1960s was for the Clary family, one of her son Matthew's friends, who requested a portrait of their two children.[58] The artist reveals in her master's thesis that this early success fostered her talent, but also helped her realize traditional portraiture was not her artistic path: "I knew nothing about the fine arts. I recall working on a portrait commission the sitter elegantly attired in front

---

[55] Matthew Clarke, "Reflections on the Garden of Eden: A Testimony in Color A Personal Biography of Jeanne Leighton-Lundberg Clarke Our Pioneer by Her Son" (unpublished manuscript, 2016), Chapter 3.
[56] Ibid.
[57] Matthew Clarke, Interview by Rebekah Monahan, November 9, 2013.
[58] Ibid.

of me and my thinking that this was a most ridiculous exercise she is sitting and me copying her."[59] She understood her preferred style would come from further training and so pursued advancement with classes at Yale University and the Silvermine Guild: "Wherever she studied, she was told that she had unusual talent. The teachers would use her work to demonstrate the ideas they were seeking to elicit from the class. It gave her first feeling of worth as a human being with something to offer other than cooking and scrubbing."[60]

This positive feedback undoubtedly assisted her drive to become an artist. The outward encouragement fulfilled portions of her life that were underrepresented. Eventually, she started to explore the art world further and began working towards her final maximalized family scenes,[61] the beginnings of which she discovered while summering in Cape Cod with her family. Reflected in even the wallpaper designs she purchased, Leighton-Lundberg delved into color and pattern. Her 1972 still lifes mark the first bright, bold, patterned style that she would become known for.[62] It seemed Leighton-Lundberg had to figure the composition of her life before she could arrange the formal qualities of the canvas. It was not the easiest venture to develop her education and style, but she continued to pursue and progress.

After her marriage ended, Leighton-Lundberg decided to regain what her previous life had neglected to offer her. She decided where to live and what to do. Shortly after moving across the country, she began studying at the major university of her Mormon religion, Brigham Young University (BYU), focusing on color and activity in her works, and completed her Bachelor of Fine Arts exhibition in December of 1977.[63] Leighton-Lundberg solidified her recognizable style and evolved in the Utah art scene. As previously mentioned, she followed with her Master of Arts in 1980, which she titled "A Considered Proposition of Reality: The Maximum Statement."[64] Leighton-Lundberg had finally completed the degrees she had abandoned in Chicago and was becoming a working artist, a path that presented a considerable challenge in 1980s Utah.

Second-wave feminism, a two-decade period acknowledged for practiced inequalities, met with considerable hostility in conservative Utah, the headquarters of the Church of Jesus Christ of Latter-day Saints (LDS). During an era when female artists still struggled for representation and respect within the contemporary art circles of New York and Los Angeles, those working in Utah, a state known for its traditional family values and strict views on gender, would have encountered an additional set of challenges. Female beauty was, in many ways, prescribed by the religious values of the region. This would have been particularly true for an artist who attended and graduated from Brigham Young University, an LDS institution. Yet,

---

[59] Jeanne Lundberg Clarke, "A Considered Proposition of Reality: The Maximum Statement" (Master of Fine Arts Thesis, Brigham Young University, 1980), 24.
[60] Matthew Clarke, "Reflections on the Garden of Eden," chapter 9.
[61] Clarke, "A Considered Proposition of Reality: The Maximum Statement," 1.
[62] Matthew Clarke, "Reflections on the Garden of Eden," chapter 10.
[63] Ibid.
[64] Clarke, "A Considered Proposition of Reality: The Maximum Statement," i.

Leighton-Lundberg did not shy away from the true complexities of female life and beauty.

MERGING HISTORIES: FEMALE FIGURES

Historically, a large collection of female "portraits" comprises an unequal share in the canon of visual arts. As subjects of imagery, it's nothing new to hear that female figures have been utilized countless times to convey beauty, sometimes celebrated and sometimes objectified. Regardless, the female body is on display. "The reclining or semi reclining female nude had long been a favorite motif of painters since Titian, whose Venus of Urbino became a reference point for nineteenth-century painters of the nude."[65]

The manner by which these previous forms of reclining females were portrayed completely reflected the artist's and the society's views of women. Nineteenth-century artists like Courbet created subjective "modest maidens."[66] Though multiple examples of these figures are not given as much agency as Leighton-Lundberg's ladies, both iterations find themselves surrounded by nature as a metaphor for womanhood and abundance. The "modest maidens" are even sometimes sleeping and unaware of their voyeurs. In these, "The sensuous abandon of the pose and the girl's obvious vulnerability invite a voyeuristic response, which may reflect [the artist's] own youthful sexuality. In such lush, verdant surroundings, we view this female form as part of the setting, as sharing in the burgeoning, organic fecundity of the forest nook which surrounds and protects her."[67] The simple fact that Leighton-Lundberg's reclining ladies are invested in the viewers can return their agency and separate her paintings from many nineteenth-century traditions. Her "Reclining Figures" look as though they commissioned and requested the portraits, as active subjects of the work. The scenes are not caught moments fabricated to place bodies on view; they are carefully crafted representations. Even though they may be generically faced, each of Leighton-Lundberg's figures seems individual; they seem to matter.

It is important to distinguish the type of idealism represented in the "Reclining Figures." Far removed from the earlier objectified female body depicted by male artists throughout art history, Leighton-Lundberg's feminine portraits represent positive attributes and an ideal projection. Each characteristic seems ready to unveil value. Firstly, their uniform representation signals a prototype in the artist's mind, a representative entity encompassing a particular ideal. Navigating layers finds the green, modest floral dress, beautifully coifed hair and face, reclined pose, and serene expression. Individually, these attributes stall at routine female beauty markers. In concert, the markers relate deeply to representations of internal qualities. The "Reclining Figures" can then be understood as the artist's ideal morals and values,

---

[65] Wendy Nolan Joyce, "Sculpting the Modern Muse: Auguste Clesinger's Femme piquee par un serpent" *Nineteenth-Century French Studies*, Col. 35, No. 1 (2006): 170, accessed November 19, 2014, DOI: 10.1353/ncf.2006.0048.
[66] Ibid.
[67] Ibid.

presented outwardly. If this woman is truly representative of what Leighton-Lundberg hoped for, she is both reflected and idealized.

In all the ways that passive nudes do not represent potential, these portraits invite questioning. Their bodies are entirely covered, leaving only the face and hands exposed. Everything else is patterned color. The face's beauty and expression anchor the chaos and garners the view. Shifting the focus from body to person neutralizes the potential for sexualization and "frustrates voyeurism."[68] Leighton-Lundberg's work is seeking a long-term relationship with viewers, not a one-night stand.

Friends saw the romanticized women clad in patterns and flowers as Leighton-Lundberg's true spirit or persona.[69] The woman is on display, but not at all objectified. Beauty and femininity stare back at the viewer, and these characteristics are from and for her, not anyone else. She is not helpless, but content with her role, and understands her place in the world. This almost romantic series of beautiful, "Reclining Figures" and mothers and daughters are a much better role to consider Leighton-Lundberg in than the other painted possibilities of fading silhouettes or those locked in anxious conversation.

Similarly, contemporary artist Mickalene Thomas represents female figures with a great deal of presence. Her work is strikingly alike, placing seated and reclining women in domestic settings, and exploring their place within contemporary society. Leighton-Lundberg's and Thomas's creation periods nearly overlap, and their parallels are both visual and conceptual. Thomas's photographic works used to make collages and paintings share Leighton-Lundberg's layered and varied backgrounds and patterns. Thomas's women also seem symbolic, carrying more than their likenesses, and appearing with more detail than the "Reclining Figures" series. Thomas's "space-age domestics or mother Africa soul searchers of her odalisque photos are draped over sofas and swathed in layers of 'exotic' prints a porn trope as much as it was a fact of '70s interior design."[70] The printed layers continue onto their bodies through tiered necklaces and painted nails, more actively incorporating them into the scenes and maintaining a stronger sense of self. While both artists are concerned with flipping the script on the art historical objectification of women, Thomas's individuals claim the frame, whereas Leighton-Lundberg's figures blend in and enhance the setting.

Both Leighton-Lundberg and Thomas use flattened figures, sometimes referencing canonical poses, to comment on a woman's role in history and society. The artists and the figures want to direct the discussion back to the gallery of people viewing their works, and they go about this in varying manners. Where Leighton-Lundberg many times rejected the feminist categorization, Thomas uses it to fuel her images. Her visuals address the treatment of African American women and incorporate more lenses than Leighton-Lundberg's paintings, perhaps speaking more strongly to the audience than the posed questions of the latter.

---

[68] Ibid.
[69] Sharon Gray, Interview by Rebekah Monahan (June 20, 2014).
[70] Kara Walker, "Mickalene Thomas," *BOMB Magazine*, April 1, 2009, https://bombmagazine.org/articles/mickalene-thomas/.

Thomas's spectacularly colorful and decorative images explore pictorial strategies around African American women, taking on such themes as femininity, celebrity, sexuality, and power, while simultaneously sending up the Blaxploitation aesthetics of 1970s black visual culture. This is achieved through cultivation of an effective tension between her painterly investments in discourses of form and the inevitable moral thicket of engaging representation of the black body. [71]

Their bodily representations put both artists in the same conversation, and their works are very intrinsically similar, composing figure, background, and concept while at the same time addressing themes of the 1970s and 1980s. Leighton-Lundberg painted within those decades, and Thomas comments on representations during that period with her contemporary body of work. It seems Thomas's pieces are a deeper continuation of what Leighton-Lundberg wanted to visualize.

In a larger sense, these artists' experiences as women are mirrored, but more easily grouped and related because of gender. Leighton-Lundberg hesitated to resign herself to an exclusively female label. She did not want to be placed into a singular category, and hers may have been an even stronger aversion, as Utah's very gendered scenarios have been echoing since pioneer times. The state's relationship with "the concepts of domestic spheres and gender roles are significant in understanding the role women played as artists during the nineteenth century in Utah because they help define the limitations and parameters of the world in which they produced their art."[72] And this pervasive filter has lasted centuries. So, Leighton-Lundberg rejected the assignment of female artist, which she understandably thought was limiting. Interestingly, this label has become a supportive review of her work and acts to enhance her representations of "Reclining Figures."

Ultimately, the formal elements within the "Reclining Figures" portraits represent Leighton-Lundberg's personality, summing up to more than a painted figure defined by gender. The bold and commanding colors relate to how those she loved remember her. The patterns represent her experiences. She shares, "My life has been so complicated there was one pattern wending its way into and through another. It becomes textural."[73] The layers tell her story.

Leighton-Lundberg's narrative tendencies verge on documentary practices, though through examples of how she thought life should be. Her practice of extending the scenes to the very edge of the canvas, and then beyond, incorporating decorative additions like flowers and repeating dots to simple frames made the liminal wood border almost fluid. Her hope was for the symbols and lessons to seep past, into the surrounding walls. The frame's duality, containing her works and yet allowing the

---

[71] Derek Conrad Murray, "Mickalene Thomas Afro-Kitsch and the Queering of Blackness" *American Art*, Vol. 28, No. 1 (2014): 10.
[72] Martha Sonntag Bradley-Evans, "Women in the Arts: Evolving Roles and Diverse Expressions," in *Women in Utah History*, ed. Patricia Lyn Scott, Linda Thatcher, Susan Allred Whetstone (University Press of Colorado, Utah State University Press, 2005), 328.
[73] Saleh, "A Feminist-Symbolist," 28.

paintings to become more familiar with their surroundings questions the function of the mitered moldings.

Of course, the frame can either operate to quietly support a work of art or ornately enhance an image as a partner. When multiple works come together in exhibition and display settings, these edges become even more important in keeping the visual and conceptual elements to themselves. In the crowded salon hangings of the past, the heavy ornate frames did this well. Here, many times, "The golden frame acts as a metonymical reference to the artwork, framing it as art. Through the association with precious materials such as gold, the more ornately carved and gilded the frame, the more valuable the viewer is led to believe the painting to be." [74] In her way, Leighton-Lundberg's painted adornment on her frames also signals value, attention to detail, and near refusal to finish the piece.

Regarding Leighton-Lundberg's career, her work ethic can be discovered while looking through slides of her works, summing up to over one hundred pieces. She was a prolific artist, and even her finished pieces were second, third, or sometimes fourth versions of themselves. Her penchant for reworking was astonishing, as she meticulously changed the color, shape or size of the most minute details, which she would sometimes refer to as "bringing the pattern up." [75] A look through her sketchbooks reveals small studies and trials that resemble wallpaper swatches or color charts. However exhaustive, these skills made her work appealing and instantly recognizable. Viewing Leighton-Lundberg's work means living her values. Her take on life, food, families, and even clothing were illustrated in oil, and the colorful scenes hint at her influence beyond their creation.

NOURISHMENT: FULFILLMENT AND SUPPORT

The theme of nourishment is paramount in Leighton-Lundberg's life and work. Perhaps the absence of support from some of her key relationships strengthened her expression of its importance. It was lacking in her childhood home and especially throughout her marriage, so Leighton-Lundberg strived to provide support to her children and grandchildren. Her strong beliefs and meticulous artistic process translate life lessons and remind viewers that careful treatment helps things grow.

For example, her 1986 painting, *Woman in Green and Red* presents a reclining figure wearing a baby's breath wreath in her hair, pearls around her neck, and is covered by oversized bouquets near her torso (fig. 5). The beautiful woman is healthy and lounges amidst a carefully laid out scene. This cross section of budding life retells viewers of the efforts needed to raise flowers and develop precious stones. Growth develops through time and attention.

---

[74] Bente Kiilerich, "Savedoff, Frames, and Parergonality," *The Journal of Aesthetics and Art Criticism* 59, no. 3 (2001): 321, http://www.jstor.org/stable/432331.
[75] Sharon Gray, Interview with Rebekah Monahan, 20 June 2014.

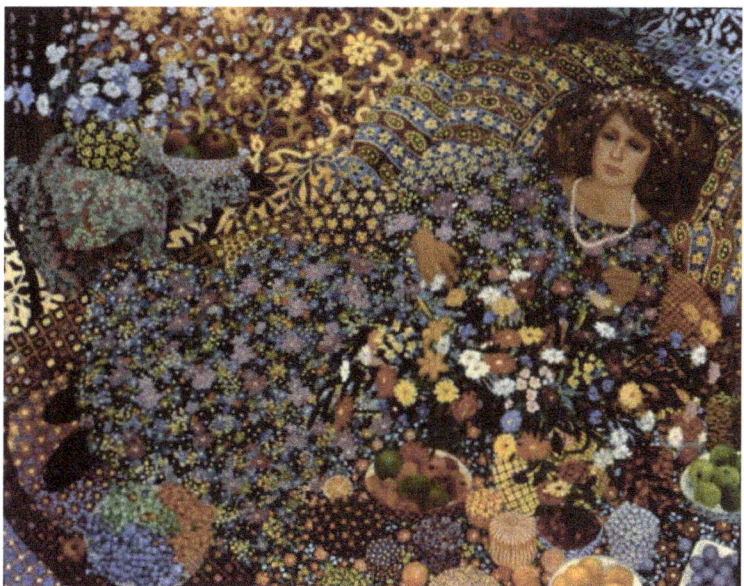

Fig. 5. Jeanne Leighton-Lundberg, *Woman in Green and Red*, 1986. Private Collection.
Source: Courtesy the Jeanne Leighton-Lundberg Clarke Family Trust

Leighton-Lundberg wanted the best out of life, especially concerning her family. She was the matriarch to her children and grandchildren, instilling in them her beliefs and life lessons. She was an animated, loving, and very opinionated figure fit to lead and inspire. She taught three grandchildren how to paint, had an insatiable desire to learn, and openly shared her views on food and nutrition;[76] an essential component of her work. Leighton-Lundberg advocated eating well and set the tables in her paintings as a metaphor for life; the best, most nourishing food was set at the center while sweets and empty calories lined the edges. "The good things in life are worth the reach."[77] These symbolic messages helped her family enjoy fulfilling lives.

Her pushy yet enduring nutritional advice is a quality that many still remember about her. And in actuality, Leighton-Lundberg may have been ahead of the curve by placing importance on what we put in our bodies. Her early still lifes contained bowls of fruit set against those patterned backdrops and in pairing the two, a visual interest in working good foods into family life comes to light. This is something that could have easily been lost on a family coming of age in a culture and time of abundant resources and novice standards set by government agencies. In fact, regulations on food came to be during the decades her art was created. When Leighton-Lundberg was experimenting with color in the late twentieth century, the Food and Drug Administration (FDA) also started paying attention to it. The 1960s mark the first-time color additives were subject to safety requirements, and the 1970s brought

---

[76] Clarke Funeral Service (Eulogies, Provo, UT, March 1, 2014).
[77] Ibid.

nutritional information to the forefront of consumer culture.[78] During that decade, the FDA worked to connect consumers to such essential knowledge, details that Leighton-Lundberg had already established as important.

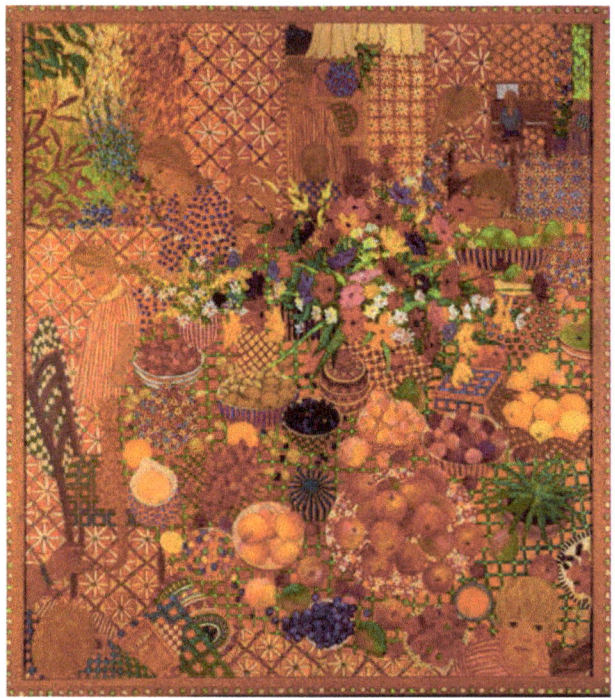

Fig. 6. Jeanne Leighton-Lundberg, *Family in Red with Piano*, 1982.
Utah Valley University Woodbury Art Museum, Orem, Utah.
Source: Courtesy the Jeanne Leighton-Lundberg Clarke Family Trust.

Looking at the details in her large works, Leighton-Lundberg incorporates nature and growth in most of her pieces. There is not a portrait without a vase of flowers or a table without fruit. She called on the viewer to, "consider the salutary life: shared moments, familial associations, the abundance of earth's provisions and man's responsibility as nurturer and preserver of the earth. Like a good companion a painting should be full of positive implications—representations of the best of life."[79] In her life, she enjoyed growing plants and being in nature. Leighton-Lundberg was an avid gardener and regularly tended to her Provo backyard. Some flowers are associated with her immediate relatives, as her daughter Susan fondly remembered the rhododendrons and forsythia of the childhood home in Connecticut and her father had

---

[78] "Regulating Cosmetics, Devices, and Veterinary Medicine After 1938," Accessed February 13, 2015, http://www.fda.gov/AboutFDA/WhatWeDo/History/Origin/ucm055137.html.
[79] Clarke, "A Considered Proposition of Reality: The Maximum Statement," 4.

loved gardenias.[80] In her works, many of the paintings include a window to what might be her teeming, beautiful garden (fig. 6). Friends understood her garden to be an extension of Leighton-Lundberg herself.[81] Her paintings' very "exterior" interiors can be explained symbolically of course (as fruits represent abundance and plants equate to life), but these details also hold a wildness that counters the careful, repetitive patterns. It is not hard to compare a spirited person to untamed nature, and Leighton-Lundberg cultivates the plants, arranges the flowers and harvests the fields in paint.

LEGACY: INFLUENCE AND FAMILY

Jeanne Leighton-Lundberg's life was full and like her art, challenged boundaries, extending to the very frame. She had a family life, an artist's life, and a teacher's life. Leighton-Lundberg's work was used for numerous publication covers and campaigns and currently exists in multiple private and museum collections. She completed many commissions for collectors around the country and was represented by galleries in Utah and California. She was invited to and included in various exhibitions, like an early show in Aspen, Colorado and a notable one-woman show at the Springville Museum of Art in 1992. Her fame exceeded the confines of Utah Valley as she was referenced internationally through her inclusion in various magazine publications. Her "Favorite Ladies" have graced "Art in the World" published by Holt, Reinhardt and Winston.[82] Leighton-Lundberg's work is selected because of its visual impact and ability to lend context.

Unfortunately, signs of Alzheimer's disease began to manifest in Leighton-Lundberg during the 1990s. Though her painting days were nearing an end, at one-point Leighton-Lundberg did express a feeling of completion prior to succumbing to the disease. She told family members she had painted everything she needed to,[83] showing control of her legacy.

As time passed, Leighton-Lundberg began to revisit her life's work in her altered state, signaling a needed intervention by family members. It was decided that many of her works would be stored at a local institution, the Woodbury Gallery, to preserve the artist's original foundation and talents. Moving the pieces to the (now) Woodbury Art Museum further opened them to the public.

The legacy continues with her children. Her late daughter Susan painted the frames of her pieces, working in tandem with Leighton-Lundberg to adorn them further with patterns and colors. And maybe even more noteworthy, her son Matthew has started his own venture in painting though he has already completed a law degree and is a university professor. Drawing inspiration from both his mother's non-traditional educational experience and her point of view, he plans on pursuing graduate studies in fine art and creating his own painting style. As his mother was

---

[80] Matthew Clarke, "Reflections on the Garden of Eden."
[81] Clarke Funeral Service.
[82] Saleh, "A Feminist-Symbolist," 28.
[83] Matthew Clarke, Interview by Rebekah Monahan, November 9, 2013.

reacting against the minimalists, Matthew has taken his cue from where Leighton-Lundberg left off, but he is working in scenes of sparser living spaces and more muted colors. He feels her work "is just so brilliantly colorful. That I'm thinking I would like to do that but in a more subtler way,"[84] from what he feels is a more masculine point of view. Perhaps seeing his work is the truest narration of her significance. The artist's son cannot create without referencing the most influential artist he knows. The next table is set.

---

[84] Ibid.

CHAPTER 3

Family Life

Jeanne Leighton-Lundberg created family themed paintings throughout much of her professional career, which stretched from about 1979 to 1991. While not an officially named series like "Favorite Ladies," the "Family Life" paintings merit discussion as a category of her work based on the similarity of structure and subject matter of the two dozen paintings. It is her largest series. Featuring seemingly mundane snapshots of everyday life, the figures pause in-situ, as they cook, read, talk, and play the piano enveloped by a variety of vividly colored patterns. While an entire spectrum of colors is present, the mood in each painting is ruled by only one or two, with yellows and reds being particularly prevalent (see *Family in Blue*, fig. 2, and *Mother in Child in Red*, fig. 7). Generally, the titles in this series are variations of numbers and colors, like *Woman and Family in Blue* or *Family in Red IV*, revealing how the pigment acts as a theme, literally coloring the canvases in one shade or another. Drenched in symbolism as thoroughly as they are saturated in color and pattern, the "Family Life" series melds genre painting and cubism in a truly maximalist method, which in turn serves to convey Leighton-Lundberg's messages about life, relationships, and religion.

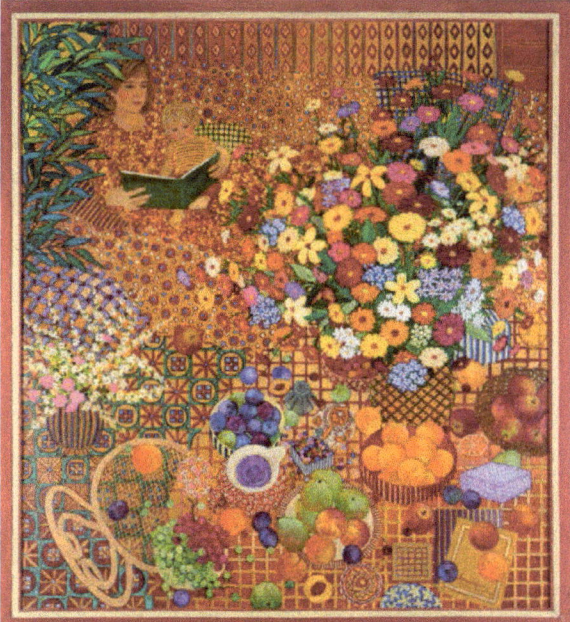

Fig. 7. Jeanne Leighton-Lundberg, *Mother and Child in Red*, 1980.
Utah Valley University Woodbury Art Museum, Orem, Utah.
Source: Courtesy the Jeanne Leighton-Lundberg Clarke Family Trust.

A Cubist Genre Scene

Usually centered around an abundantly laid table, Leighton-Lundberg allows viewers to peer through her patterns into kitchens and living rooms, catching glimpses of mothers, fathers, and children engaged in the normal rituals of family life. Rather than posing the figures in one room, Leighton-Lundberg has applied a fractured, cubist-like perspective to the genre-based subject matter of home and family. She maximalizes the viewer's experience of family by painting tops of heads, profiles, and a variety of actions as individual members engage in a division of family labor. But rather than using a single, wide angle perspective typical of most genre paintings, Leighton-Lundberg has distorted and flattened the scene using multiple perspectives that coalesce to break down the walls of the home. Through this technique her paintings reveal simultaneous activities, which in actuality, would be completed separately. Leighton-Lundberg's bold use of brightly colored patterns serves at once to energize the scene and to exacerbate the flatness, voiding the rooms of shadow and depth in a manner much more modern than the genre themes her family life scenes first call to mind. Thus, an analysis of Leighton-Lundberg's "Family Life" series requires comparison to two very different movements in art history: the subject matter brings to mind American genre paintings, particularly those of the American antebellum, while the bright colors, flatness, and distorted perspective are more closely aligned with synthetic cubism of the 1930s.

Like the genre painters in the nineteenth century who captured a broad view of American life, the paintings in Leighton-Lundberg's "Family Life" series reflect many similar themes. The nineteenth century represented a transformative period for the newly formed nation during which westward expansion, increased industrialization, suffrage, abolition, and politics surrounding the Civil War played major roles. From depictions of home, family, and rural community life to more complex political topics like the relationship between blacks and whites, economic disparity between classes, and the role of women,[85] the genre paintings of this period reflect fundamental national values and the development of American identity. As the nation grew, population and wealth increased, and the art market in America became more diversified, with "auction houses, art lotteries, and fly-by-night dealers"[86] opening in many cities, allowing artists to break free of their dependence on portrait commissions and expand their subjects of interest to appeal to wider audiences. This newly energized art market escalated artistic competition, opening the profession to more artists, including women like Lilly Martin Spencer (1822-1902), whose unique insider perspective cast a critical eye on the domestic sphere.[87]

One of the most popular genre painters of the American antebellum, Lilly Martin Spencer's work focused mainly on themes of home and family using airy light, a palette of bright pigments, and jovial undertones of wit and confidence. She

---

[85] Weinberg, H. Barbara, and Carrie Rebora Barratt. "American Scenes of Everyday Life, 1840–1910." In Heilbrunn Timeline of Art History. New York: The Metropolitan Museum of Art, 2000–. http://www.metmuseum.org/toah/hd/scen/hd_scen.htm (September 2009)
[86] Ibid.
[87] Ibid.

presented the lives of women as adoring, affectionate mothers and capable, hardworking housekeepers, making "the urban middle-class mother into something of a secular saint."[88] In the 1850s Spencer filled her sketchbooks with dreamy depictions of women holding babies, watching over sleeping children, and doting on cherubic toddlers, conveying the conservative ideals of motherhood and even calling to mind depictions of the Madonna and Child with her simple yet intimate figural arrangement and composition.[89] Similar subject matter is also found in the work of Jeanne Leighton-Lundberg, albeit in a vastly different presentation.

Where Spencer's figures dominate the paintings as subjects in their own right, Leighton-Lundberg's hide on the periphery, only emerging from the eye-popping maximalist canvas under careful scrutiny. In contrast to Lilly Martin Spencer's optically accurate style which draws viewers through the depths of the paintings with rich colors, bright light, and contrasting shadows, Leighton-Lundberg's families exist in shallow, confined spaces, boxed in by patterns which emphasize their two-dimensionality, as broken planes compete equally for prominence. Where Spencer's airy paintings convey a sense of dimension through the exquisite use of light and shadow, Leighton-Lundberg's paintings are free of this modeling. In *Family in Red with Piano* (fig. 6), Leighton-Lundberg's figures emerge out of the patterns, initially camouflaged by the color-saturated designs of their clothing. On the left, a young girl stands on a chair pulled out from the table while the mother plaits the child's blonde hair. Seven other characters surface from the undulating waves of stripes and florals, with size difference providing the only clues to depth in an almost perspectiveless room. Despite these differences, the themes of family harmony and traditional roles for women are found in both Spencer's and Leighton-Lundberg's work. Although painted more than a century later, Leighton-Lundberg's depictions of the relationships between mothers and children reflects the same love and doting attention present in Spencer's work.

Interestingly, while both women's paintings depict mothers in traditional, heteronormative roles, both Spencer and Leighton-Lundberg led rather unconventional lives for women of their times. Spencer, born in 1822, was encouraged by her progressive parents to not only pursue an education but also to enter the public sphere as a career artist. Balancing her role as sole breadwinner with that of mother to her thirteen children (seven of whom lived to adulthood) and wife, Spencer supported her family while her husband encouraged her career and took on many responsibilities of the home.[90] Yet rather than embodying the challenge to middle class patriarchy posed by nineteenth century feminists, as one might expect of someone with her background, Spencer's depictions of home life were radically conservative, upholding the traditional role of women in the family[91] and bringing her

---

[88] Elizabeth Johns, *American Genre Painting: The Politics of Everyday Life*, Yale University Press, 1993: 174.
[89] Ibid.
[90] Seeing America Through Artists' Eyes, Memorial Art Gallery, University of Rochester https://mag.rochester.edu/seeingAmerica/pdfs/10.pdf
[91] Katz, Wendy Jean. *Regionalism and Reform: Art and Class Formation in Antebellum Cincinnati.* Columbus: Ohio State University Press, 2002.

work under critical scrutiny for "its sentimental rhetoric deifying motherly nurture, the beauty of domesticity, and the homey humor of family life" making her "complicit with furthering or "reproducing" systems of domination of mid nineteenth-century American women."[92] She did not paint women outside the realm of femininity but rather specialized in painting domestic genre scenes that often depicted women in the midst of household duties such as preparing meals, as seen in *Young Wife: First Stew* (1854) and *Peeling Onions* (1852), or caring for children, reflected in *This Little Piggy Went to Market* (1857). Like many genre painters of the time, Spencer recorded the lives of women as "devoted mothers, dedicated household managers, participants in genteel feminine rituals, and resolute keepers of culture."[93] Similarly, Leighton-Lundberg favored subjects related to women, families, and traditional home life, placing her themes squarely in the realm of genre painting, despite her life not fitting the mold of typical for a woman born in the 1920s. As was discussed in chapter two, Leighton-Lundberg attended several years of college in the 1940s at a time when only 1% of women in the United States held college degrees and female employment was on the decline due to post-War economics.[94] Although she did not graduate at that time, she continued to pursue her education informally and eventually moved across the country to complete what she had started decades earlier. Already in her 50s and twice divorced, Leighton-Lundberg put herself through college and graduate school, completing her MFA in 1980 and placing herself in the minority of less than 14% of women holding at least a four-year college degree.[95] Both Spencer, painting during the First Wave of the Feminist Movement, and Leighton-Lundberg, painting during the Second Wave, participated in non-traditional roles, yet chose to paint women fulfilling traditional responsibilities and the details of everyday life in a domestic sphere rather than pushing the boundaries of acceptable roles for women. Despite the similarity of themes and subject matter, a side-by-side look at one of Spencer's and Leighton-Lundberg's paintings reveals major differences in style and technique.

Rather than the preciseness of a single viewpoint used in nineteenth century genre paintings, the use of mixed perspective in Leighton-Lundberg's work reveals a bird's-eye view of the figures and table in the lower thirds of the painting, while the figures and objects in the upper third exist in profile or portrait—the composition remaining extraordinarily non-disjointed, as if the room exists on a shallow curve. While the table exists in the foreground, the space between it and the back wall is visually very short, emphasizing the intimacy of the environment. It is this flattening and fracturing of perspective that draws comparison to the still lifes of synthetic

---

[92] David M. Lubin, "Picturing a Nation: Art and Social Change in Nineteenth-century America." Yale University Press, 1994: 161.
[93] Ibid.
[94] Madeline Chisholm, "Women, Marriage, Education, and Occupation in the United States from 1940-2000," Dartmouth College, Novemeber 2016, https://journeys.dartmouth.edu/censushistory/2016/11/03/women-marriage-and-education-in-the-united-states-from-1940-2000/
[95] Thomas D. Snyder, editor, "120 Years of American Education: A Statistical Portrait," Center for Education Statistics. U.S. Department of Education. 1993:8. https://nces.ed.gov/pubs93/93442.pdf

cubism. Both *Still Life with* Newspaper (1916) by Juan Gris and *Mandolin and Guitar* (1924) by Pablo Picasso are good examples of the flatness and perspectivelessness that Leighton-Lundberg sought to accomplish. Synthetic cubism differs from analytic cubism in that the artists abandoned the analysis of objects in favor of "constructing" or "synthesizing" [objects] through the overlapping of larger, more discrete forms that seemed as if they might have been cut and pasted to the canvas. This new form of Cubism, which featured brighter colors, ornamental patterns, undulating lines, and rounded as well as jagged shapes, was common into the 1930s. [96] Leighton-Lundberg's paintings are like inhabited cubist still lifes, the compositions made even more complicated by dizzying patterns and eye-popping colors, while the subject matter is contrastingly flat. In her thesis, Leighton-Lundberg wrote that she sought to "synthesize the avant-garde tendency for an over-simplified, severely abstract, two-dimensional, non-figurative color-field work and a restatement of the more traditional genre painting element,"[97] no simple task. It was with this goal in mind that she applied a maximalist use of pattern and color to the figurative elements in order to maintain a flattened schemata.[98]

In stark contrast to the purposeful abstractions of cubism, it is the use of subtle tones, mastery of visual texture, and Spencer's ability to capture exquisitely lifelike, and occasionally comical, facial expressions that allowed for a composition that is a portrait first, and record of human activity second.[99] Likewise, Leighton-Lundberg's compositions are maximalist painting first, and depiction of family life second. The symbolic supersedes the representational aspects of her work. Spencer's attentive eye is demonstrated in the accurately depicted details of dress and gesture in her paintings of familial interactions. They speak to direct observation and indeed Spencer drew much inspiration from her own home, often using herself and her children as models. In the same vein, Leighton-Lundberg's depictions of family life could assumedly have been taken from interactions with or observations of her own family. The complexity and originality of both artists speaks to an interest in the importance of human interactions in daily life. Furthermore, Leighton-Lundberg's "Family Life" paintings play with concepts of time (moments versus eternity) and attempt to educate viewers, both of which are efforts shared by genre painters of centuries past.

Importantly, it was the dilemma of representing the fourth dimension—time—which led to the birth of Cubism, that ties the cubists to the American genre painters of the nineteenth century. The predicament explored by the cubists was how to represent the ever-shifting reality of time as the human consciousness experiences it. [100] The medium of oil on canvas lends itself to capturing fleeting

---

[96] "Cubism." Guggenheim Collection Online, Solomon R. Guggenheim Foundation, Accessed December 30, 2017. <www.guggenheim.org/artwork/movement/cubism>
[97] Jeanne Lundberg Clarke, "A Considered Proposition of Reality: The Maximum Statement." Master's thesis, Brigham Young University, 1980.
[98] Ibid. at 8.
[99] Seeing America Through Artists' Eyes, Memorial Art Gallery, University of Rochester https://mag.rochester.edu/seeingAmerica/pdfs/10.pdf
[100] Ninón Rodríguez, "Cubism: A New Vision," Miami Dade College, n.d. Web. Accessed December 20, 2017, https://www.mdc.edu/wolfson/Academic/ArtsLetters/art_philosophy/Humanities/Cubism/cubism%20front2.htm.

moments much more readily than the dynamic, changing vision of Picasso or Braque. However, they managed to solve the conundrum by "fragment[ing] objects and pictorial space into semitransparent, overlapping, faceted planes of pigment, thought by some to show the spatial shift from different perspectives within the same time and space and to emphasize the canvas's real two-dimensional flatness instead of conveying the illusory appearance of depth."[101] In a similar vein, Leighton-Lundberg applied rhythmic paisleys and repetitions of shapes to her canvases to emphasis the visual flatness and play with the idea of eternity as it applies to familial relationships. While she was less interested in the way an object's appearance changes according to the perspective from which it is viewed, she did use the technique of flattened spatial relations to convey changing points of view of the whole room. The compressed picture plane causes objects and people to lose their concreteness; the table melds into the floor, the figures sink into the walls, and suddenly the whole has taken precedence over the sum of its parts. This merger of genre painting and cubism as executed by Leighton-Lundberg is Maximalism. But in order to understand fully what she sought to accomplish with the "Family Life" series, one must also dissect the purpose of her patterns and her use of symbolism in the series.

PATTERN THEORY

Perhaps more so than her other paintings, the "Family Life" series is indicative of Leighton-Lundberg's pattern theory. A mother bakes, parents read to their children, extended family gather for a meal, a grandmother speaks to a smiling child resting on her knee; depictions of familial interactions placed within the context of a myriad of overlapping paisleys, geometric boarders, and floral designs. While the intense use of pattern is part of her maximalist approach, it does more than colorfully fill the canvas. These visual repetitions reflect Leighton-Lundberg's interest in the patterning of the traditions and routines of life, together amounting to a very personal, overarching pattern theory: "My life has been so complicated—a bad marriage and lots of things dumping on me all at once. There was one pattern wending its way into and through another."[102] For Leighton-Lundberg, patterns don't just appear as a series of events that occur in one's life. Rather, patterns function on both minute and grand scales to rule existence. From the arrangement of nitrogenous bases in a person's genetic code, to the routines and habits that direct daily life, to the repetition of time and dates, Leighton-Lundberg believed that human lives are patterned in multitudinous ways. She wrote: "Pattern is in everything. Every plant has its own peculiar leaf, stem, fruit, seed, size, and shape. There is pattern in personality, voice, tradition, preference, and habit, and so on. Patterns are a birthright, an invitation, and a choice. They are everywhere present. In all of my painting I try to explain the "Idea" of living by the use of pattern."[103] In her "Family Life" series, Leighton-Lundberg portrays the

---

[101] "Cubism." Guggenheim Collection Online, Solomon R. Guggenheim Foundation, Accessed December 30, 2017, www.guggenheim.org/artwork/movement/cubism.
[102] Patricia Saleh, "A Feminist-Symbolist." Fine Art Collector International 2, no. 2 (1992): 29.
[103] Jeanne Leighton-Lundberg, "Inheritance 1." Artist Statement. Unpublished. Fall 1991.

interaction of these life-patterns both explicitly and conceptually through painted design on canvas.

Although the visual patterns are less complex and include none of the over layering present in many of the works, the painting *Inheritance 1* is a prime example of explicit pattern use in Leighton-Lundberg's "Family Life" series. In contrast to the majority of the paintings in the "Family Life" series, *Inheritance 1* shows a family sitting together on a couch, looking directly out of the canvas, as if posing for a formal portrait. Father and mother sit in the center, a young child on each lap, while an older son sits to their left holding a cat, and an older daughter sits to their right with a dog resting its head on her lap. Each article of clothing displays a distinct pattern for a dizzying effect, the figures at once separate from each other and yet blended together because of the purposeful lack of modeling and shadow. Writing of *Inheritance 1*, Leighton-Lundberg referred to the physical attributes or "looks" of the mother and father as the main theme:

> These two have joined together and have brought their patterns into their children. His patterns are shown in back of his head and are exampled in the five-petaled flowers and the diagonal diamond shape. Her patterns are at her back and are represented by the four-petaled flowers and the rectilinear square and vertical/horizontal form. Each of their patterns are seen in the children. The girls resemble their father in facial features, hair coloring, etc. The boys resemble the mother. The cat resembles the mother, the dog the father, and so on.[104]

Thus, Leighton-Lundberg's pattern making is two-fold; first, the children are "patterned" after their parents in the way their shared genetics create anatomical similarities. Secondly, the children wear the same patterns as their parents, signifying inherited preferences, talents, and predispositions, as well as learned behaviors and family traditions, which establish, to some degree, the pattern of their lives. While Leighton-Lundberg's pattern theory as it relates to familial traits is perhaps more overt in this family than others in the series, the rhythmic repetitions also function more implicitly as symbolic patterns of life and the passage of time.

Formally, the patterns in the foreground and background of *Inheritance 1* employ repetitions of geometric shapes and undulating colors to create a sense of movement—an almost mathematical routine bringing to mind the dizzying kinetic compositions of Richard Anuszkiewicz. Likewise, Leighton-Lundberg hoped that the dynamic colors and patterns surrounding the figures would convey a feeling of movement, signifying the passage of time.[105] From fleeting moments to the passing of years, the family's life is measured by the carefully timed movement of patterns— representing daily tasks as well as major milestones. The choreography of stripes, squares, dots, and flowers acts like a metronome for breakfast, lunch, dinner, and everything in between.

---

[104] Ibid.
[105] Jeanne Leighton-Lundberg, "Inheritance 1." Artist Statement. Unpublished. Fall 1991.

Family in Blue (fig. 2) further exemplifies these measured characteristics. The highly gridded walls and table are rhythmically pleasing, while the latticed floor provides a foundation for the children to the rear. The father leans against a wall in the upper left corner, with a handless clock hung almost at eye level to his left. The patterns distance the untimed acts within the scene, allowing viewers to further quantify family life. The painting remains traditional in its representation of a nuclear family, reminding us of the artist's vision for families to function as a cooperative unit. Jumping from one area of the work to another incites viewers to assess the designs and repetitions being produced inside the home, and the meticulous patterns provide a nice foil to the unconcerned clock. This back and forth results in an Escher-like evaluation of beginnings and ends.

The obsessive use of patterns, built up in layers upon layers, in the "Family Life" series serves as an invitation to viewers to sort out where one pattern starts and another end just as all beings try to make sense of life's repetitions. Paisleys, diamonds, dots, and florals electrify the walls, floors, furniture, and figures. But they also stand alone, for example in *Family in Purple and Blue* (fig. 8), in which rectangular sections of pattern jump from the walls to the foreground, ignoring rules of perspective, and becoming more than design fill. This over-layering in an important part of her work.

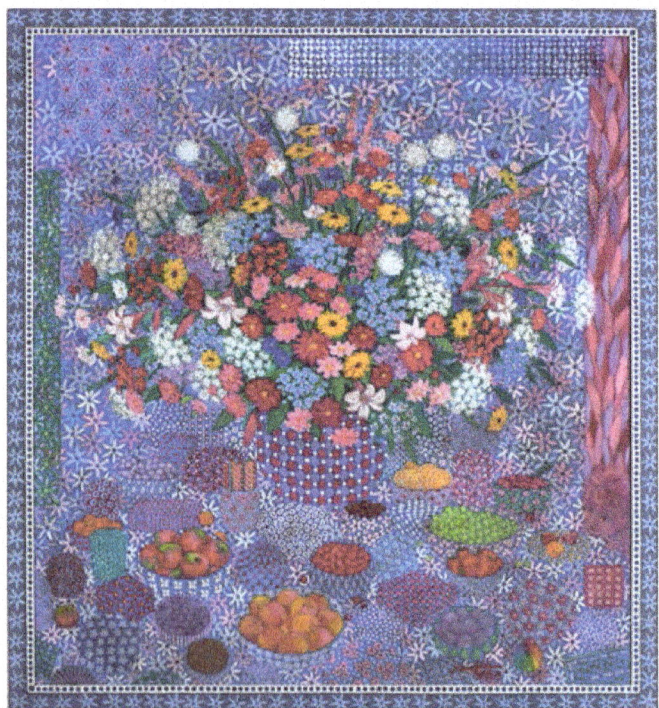

Fig. 8. Jeanne Leighton Lundberg Clarke, *Still Life: Vases and Two Faces* (1994). Springville Museum of Art (Springville, Utah).
Source: Courtesy the Springville Museum of Art.

Significantly, Leighton-Lundberg's process involved reworking sections of her paintings over and over, sometimes re-coloring and re-patterning an entire canvas over the course of several years until she was satisfied. This approach reveals an interest in dissecting competing patterns, in an artistic nature-versus-nurture debate. Leighton-Lundberg staunchly believed that while genetic code and upbringing may predispose a person to certain things, there is always an aspect of agency, stating that, "life is not chance; it is choice."[106] This speaks to her belief that even patterns that people believe they are "locked into" can be redefined according to evolving "perceptions and attitudes."[107] Here she is most certainly alluding to particular patterns in her upbringing: the habits, genetics, and predispositions she inherited from her parents. Without a doubt, her upbringing combined with the experience of her own unhappy marriage was in part the catalyst for the voyeuristic scenes of warm familial relationships found in the "Family Life" series. In many ways, the "Family Life" paintings are her way of coming to terms with the distant way she was parented and an unfortunately less than ideal childhood, which she ultimately overcame through her own more involved parenting style.

Outside of art, the 1970's and 1980's hosted other factors against which to measure a family. Changes from mid-century America were documented and assessed at an increased rate, and many times families like Leighton-Lundberg's were at the core of such studies. A 1986 analysis stated that "A review of the existing literature suggests several sources of variation in susceptibility to depression among full-time housewives: socio-demographic characteristics, family life cycle variables, extent of social isolation or social integration outside the home, and satisfaction with the role."[108] Arguably, clues to Leighton-Lundberg's feelings about or status within these dimensions can be found within this series of paintings. Other burgeoning developments like women's movements and shifting politics must have been present somewhere in the artist's mind during their creation. However, these ideas were external assessments crafted by researcher's contemporary to the "Family Life" series. For a more introspective review, Leighton-Lundberg looked to religion. Her self-reflective statements reveal a belief in the principle of agency, or free-will, an important component of her Mormon faith, as opposed to reliance on fate or predestination.

Religious Symbolism in the "Family Life" Series

Jeanne Leighton-Lundberg preferred to have her work examined outside the context of her "self," rejecting labels that sought to typecast her paintings into any particular realm, including those of woman artist, feminist artist, and Mormon artist. While she rejected those labels, Leighton-Lundberg did not shy away from styles or subject matter that would align her art with others' in those categories. Just as the "Favorite

---

[106] Jeanne Leighton-Lundberg, "Statement of Purpose." Artist Statement. Unpublished. c. 1990-1992.
[107] Jeanne Leighton-Lundberg, "Symbolist." Artist Statement. Unpublished. c. 1990-1992.
[108] Constance L. Shehan, Mary Ann Burg, and Cynthia A. Rexroat, "Depression and the Social Dimensions of the Full-Time Housewife Role," *The Sociological Quarterly*, Vol. 27 No. 3 (1986): 405.

Ladies" series is rife with feminist undertones, the "Family Life" series is undeniably focused on home and family—loaded with an abundance of motifs and patterns typically associated with Western femininity. But what is of most significance in the "Family Life" series is Leighton-Lundberg's desire not to be considered a religious or Mormon artist. Leighton-Lundberg was baptized into The Church of Jesus Christ of Latter-day Saints as an adult not long before recommencing her formal art education in 1974. While none of the works in the "Family Life" series is explicitly religious (there are no scenes of the annunciation or crucifixion), the colorfully patterned paintings are loaded with symbols, coded images, and themes revealing an exploration of religious beliefs such as the role of families, the idea of agency, and the existential notion of Truth represented by the use of color.

In keeping with her Mormon faith, Leighton-Lundberg believed that families are eternal units, created on Earth and perpetuated in the afterlife. She portrays the belief that familial relationships are of the utmost importance through the use of figures in the series. She said, "The theme I use most frequently is the family, for it is the most important communal unit ever established, a place of nurture and loving care which encourages a healthy, wholesome population."[109] A closer look at the "Family Life" figures is reflective of her belief that familial relationships are the most essential part of life[110] and serves to put the relatives in context. We see interactions, conversations, families caring for each other and playing, along with the seemingly mundane tasks of homemaking performed in the background by women. Other figures hide along the edges of the paintings, their faces partially obscured by bowls and bouquets of flowers. In some a small, dimpled hand, reaches for a piece of fruit from off scene. These hidden figures show that there is more to a family that first meets the eye. Studying the faces and poses reveals the complex emotions that are part of daily life. Happiness, sadness, joy and loneliness can be attributed to the various characters. They flicker in and out of the colors and patterns that build the world around them. The only constant element is the set table, full of the things and experiences in life that can strengthen or break relationships.

Leighton-Lundberg wrote and talked frequently of the heavily laden table, which she used to represent the world and life experience. See, for example, *Family in Red with Piano* (fig. 6). The table, flattened virtually to a point of non-perspective is bedecked with bowls of fruit and nuts, vases of flowers, and brightly covered boxes. Central to this motif is the role of agency. The many items filling the table represent various aspects of life: sweets and nuts are the "good things in life," the covered containers are uncontrollable experiences—things that cannot be anticipated—that can be good or difficult, and the fruits are a reference to the scriptural passage "by their fruits shall ye know them" (Matthew 7:20), representing the deeds and actions that each individual brings to the table. Thus, individuals bring their experiences and "gifts" to the table, which they share with others just as they partake in the things that

---

[109] Jeanne Leighton-Lundberg, "Loving Challenge" American Mothers Inc. Publication. c. 1990-1998.
[110] "Clarke, Jeanne Leighton Lundberg (1925)." Springville Museum of Art. Accessed August 5, 2016, http://www.smofa.org/collections/browse.html?x=artist&artist_id=431.

others bring. It is this shared experience in which all the people of the word are nourished and taught.

Almost incongruously, the one instrument in the family home built to measure time does not. The clocks in the "Family Life" series are left handless, symbolizing the idea that relationships formed and nurtured within the home are eternal—immune to the ravages of time. At least on the surface, these defunct objects add a peculiar air to the genre scenes when only considered within the confines of the immediate painting. But symbolically, the clocks offer an alternative idea of measurement. The timekeepers function on a much wider definition of intervals than minutes and hours, relating to Leighton-Lundberg's beliefs of an eternal family unit remaining together regardless of the consequences of time.

Beyond the representation of the tables and clocks, Leighton-Lundberg's heavy use of symbolism, which she explains in several unpublished artist's statements, can be found in every detail of the paintings. The bouquets on the tables represent the multicultural people of the world, each with its own particular form, together forming a beautiful chorus of scents and colors. Light and colors even play a symbolic role in terms of flatness and complimentary and secondary relationships. These symbols especially allude to scripture and religion. The two elements of color and light are intrinsically and spiritually linked for her, as she states white light encompasses all color: "With all the colors together you'll get white light there are no shadows. I'm a religious person, and the white light really means the light of truth."[111] While all of her works use the color spectrum in the sense that all primary and secondary colors are accounted for, several of her paintings contain an actual color spectrum painted within the image. The symbol of the color spectrum is a reminder that the painting contains all the colors together, conveying her belief that the light of truth is present in the family. This interesting mix of obvious and more obscure symbolism (an actual color spectrum versus the use of all colors on the spectrum throughout the painting), show the different ways that Leighton-Lundberg explored her religion through paint:

> I don't paint Jesus on the cross you understand, but I do try to convey a message from the human point of view by incorporating it with the idea of pattern and the choices of patterns, and the light with which color is able to be seen. Color disappears where light disappears, and in the spiritual sense life disappears when light and truth disappear. We must have understanding about the purposes of light in life and respecting it and the fact that life has the right to be nurtured and treated kindly even animals have the right to be treated with spiritual and loving insight." [112]

Thus, she did not depict literal religious scenes typically found in art history to convey messages, but instead used pattern, color, and symbolism to explore her faith and share with others her point of view.

---

[111] Patricia Saleh, "A Feminist-Symbolist," Fine Art Collector International, Vol. 2, No. 2 (1992): 31.
[112] Ibid.

Maximalism and Visual Delight

CHAPTER 4

Favorite Ladies

Arguably the most famous of Leighton-Lundberg's paintings, and undoubtedly the most iconic, are those from her "Favorite Ladies" series. The eight[113] large paintings in the series were completed between 1986 and 1992. Each features a set of 12-16 women from prominent historical paintings seated around a decadent spread of technicolored fruit, bright patterned boxes, and bowls brimming with delicacies extending to the very edge of a large round table. From Victorine, courtesy Manet's *Luncheon on the Grass* (1863) to Willem de Kooning's *Woman, I* (1950–1952), famous faces peer from Leighton-Lundberg's paintings, like a Who's Who of women in art.

Selected from the canon of art history, "the ladies are representations of women from many different centuries and cultures, who, through their images, have continued to "live" in the history of art, for all the world to see and ponder and enjoy."[114] Carefully arranged to facilitate an imagined conversation, some women look at each other while others turn to the viewers as if to implore a reason for interrupting their bounteous feast. In her statement of purpose, Leighton-Lundberg envisioned asking the women about their beliefs, upbringing, and home life, as well as any opportunities for education and happiness. Lastly, she wanted to know how, if given the chance, they would have liked to change their lives. Showing more innovation than she is often credited, her defining series incorporates strong postmodern markers (in particular an obvious appropriation of sources), a literal re-dressing of figures, and a feminist approach to the selection of included women.

APPROPRIATION AND "THE QUESTION"

Leighton-Lundberg developed her signature style during an era when contemporary art was transitioning from Post Minimalism to Post Modernism, with appropriation a particularly strong artistic trend during the 1980s. Indeed, Leighton-Lundberg's historical quotations could be interpreted as a form of readymade art, a commentary on postmodern society and identity. Although artists had been drawing references from one another's works for millennia, appropriation artists drew attention to their quotation of references: they re-photographed, repainted, and sometimes simply cut and pasted from original sources with a kind of lawless disregard for the strictures of

---

[113] At least one of the paintings documented is actually an earlier version of another (*Entertaining Favorite Ladies: Millennial* was painted over to become *Entertaining Favorite Ladies III*). Painting and over-painting (even of a completed work) was a typical part of Jeanne's process. For purposes of this paper, we will treat each documented version as a separate work.
[114] Jeanne Leighton-Lundberg, "Statement of Purpose." Artist Statement. Unpublished. c. 1990-1992.

copyright protection. And that was precisely the point. They were asking intimate questions about authenticity, originality, and media culture.

Rather than using the tool of appropriation to make a comment on the reproducibility of contemporary culture, it seems as if Leighton-Lundberg used appropriation simply to honor women of the past, women who may have been denied identification as anything other than decorative, desirable objects. In this way, she questioned the authenticity of representations of women by artists throughout history. While Leighton-Lundberg's approach differs significantly from appropriation artists like Richard Prince or Sherrie Levine, she employed a similar method of referencing recognizable images in order to ask a simple, yet poignant question: "What do you think of the way he painted me?" A question imbued with allusions of misogyny and sexism as much as artistic integrity and authenticity.

But the purpose of the series was not for Leighton-Lundberg to answer this question, but rather to set the stage for viewers to do so themselves. Leighton-Lundberg used appropriation as a line of inquiry, bringing together a dozen images from historical paintings around her classic table. As in Leighton-Lundberg's other paintings, the table represents the world and the multiplicity of experiences life brings. Usually, the various bowls of fruit represent what each person brings to the table and the closed containers the uncontrollable and unpredictable experiences that occur at every stage of life.[115] However, the "Favorite Ladies" table is a little different in that the figures represent works of art that have been influential to Leighton-Lundberg's work and development as an artist. In this case, the table is better represented as a conversation about art, in which Leighton-Lundberg is an active participant.

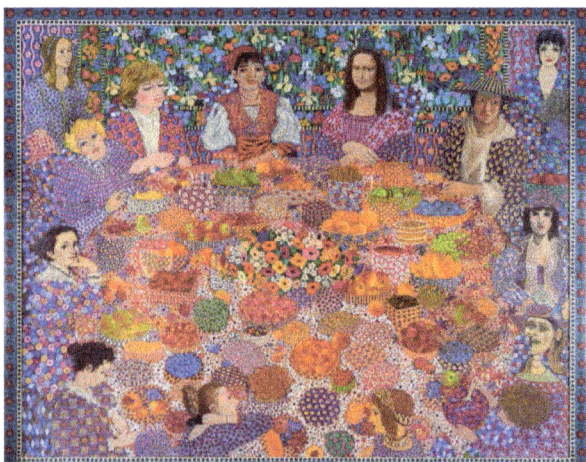

Fig. 9. Jeanne Leighton-Lundberg, *Entertaining Favorite Ladies III*, 1991.
Utah Valley University Woodbury Art Museum, Orem, Utah.
Source: Courtesy the Jeanne Leighton-Lundberg Clarke Family Trust.

---

[115] Jeanne Leighton-Lundberg, "Statement of Purpose." Artist Statement. Unpublished. c. 1990-1992.

At the table, Leighton-Lundberg presents, by way of appropriation, what each woman has to offer such as artistic style, brushwork, art movement, and the like, and also paints herself in a serving role, bringing her own contribution to the table. As she put it, "I'm trying to serve these women as they have served me."[116] Her phrasing is interesting—"trying to serve these women"—particularly because she seems to ignore the actual artist to focus instead on a product of their work. Although she recognized the influence of male artists in her art and their contributions to art history, she did not paint the male artists themselves at her table. This is not surprising, when considering Leighton-Lundberg's dislike of painting men; male figures only appear in Leighton-Lundberg's work within the context of the family, for example, *Family in Blue* (1981, fig. 2). Her knowledge of the unenviable, chauvinistic lives of many of the male artists who influenced her (particularly Picasso and de Kooning) and distrust of men in general[117] surely led her to a more creative way of paying homage to the impact their artistic contributions had on her work. After all, many of these artists became famous by painting women. For example, Renaissance man Leonardo da Vinci had a major impact on the arts and sciences, but his best-known contribution is arguably a relatively small (30 in x 21 in) painting of a woman. The *Mona Lisa* (1503) has been called "the best known, the most visited, the most written about, the most sung about, the most parodied work of art in the world."[118] Even if her actual identity cannot be agreed upon, the world can recognize Mona Lisa in parody or not. So, this question, "What do you think of the way he painted me," has perhaps already been answered for Mona Lisa.

From the interviews Leighton-Lundberg gave about her work,[119] a very likely interpretation of the "Favorite Ladies" series is that it is the women who directly inspired her rather than the men who painted them. After all, it was the women who influenced the artists originally and it is the women's faces that we see in the artist's paintings. Yet, most of these favorite ladies' names and stories are unknown and perhaps even of no interest to the audiences of today. When viewers look at these women, they see a Degas or a Vermeer rather than the woman for who and what she was. Disconnected from their original settings, Leighton-Lundberg creates a sense of ambiguity; removed of context she creates a degree of separation from their artists, freeing them to be seen for who they really are.

While her readymade figures appear at first glance to be decorative objects locked into the confines of interior space, on closer inspection one notices that her women are not passive objects at all. This reversal of objectification or repatriation of women is exactly what Leighton-Lundberg sought to remedy by bringing the women together into a single painting. The women define the interior space of the paintings: they shape it, form it, and even create it. Pattern does not appear for the sake of pattern, but to provide a visual contrast to the faces of the women, each of which

---

[116] Saleh, 30.
[117] Sharon Gray, Interview with Rebekah Monahan. June 20, 2014.
[118] John Lichfield, "The Moving of the Mona Lisa." *The Independent*. February 2, 2005. Accessed June 15, 2015. http://www.independent.co.uk/news/world/europe/the-moving-of-the-mona-lisa-6149165.html
[119] Patricia Saleh, "A Feminist-Symbolist." Fine Art Collector International, Vol. 2, No. 2 (1992), and Carol Lea Clark. "Jeanne Leighton-Lundberg," *Southwest Art Magazine*, October 1989.

reflects a different artistic style. The table is a unifying compositional device. Unlike the women of Bonnard and Matisse, who often find themselves pinned between table and wall, Leighton-Lundberg's women occupy their own space. The women do not exist simply to justify a decorative framework. And the colors do not wear the women; the women wear the colors, colors that spill from the canvas like ripe fruit and tropical blossoms, colors that ensnare the senses.

As mentioned above, the objective of the "Favorite Ladies" series is to reevaluate the way male artists have portrayed women in art. By placing the women at the table, Leighton-Lundberg invites viewers to consider the varying thought processes about women in history. When she looked at the women, she imagined them asking the question "What do you think of the way he painted me?"[120] In this way, Leighton-Lundberg takes the women, objectified in their original paintings, makes them the subject of the "Favorite Ladies" paintings, and allows them to speak for themselves.

REDRESSING: FASHION AND MODESTY

In the "Favorite Ladies" series, each woman is painted using the same style and technique of her original painter, but with some differences from the original. While remaining true to the style of dress, notable alterations have been made to the patterns and colors of each woman's clothes that reflect Leighton-Lundberg's unique flare for fashion. Indeed, she once asserted, "I'm sort of in the fashion industry too because I dress my women. Beautiful clothing was peculiar to the wealthy classes in the old days, but now we have nice looks for all incomes, so I put a little pattern into the garments in my paintings."[121] For Leighton-Lundberg, there was no such thing as fashion for fashion's sake. In her own clothing, Leighton-Lundberg's eclectic wardrobe included colorful pieces that she would wear in tandem.[122] Dressing herself was an expression of her personality—another canvas for her to paint. As a symbolist, she felt that fashion was not just a decorative addition to life. Dress and fashion are extremely personal reflections of self-identity that at the same time convey contextualization for eras, and adherence to social norms. In this way, clothing also serves as an identifying marker for many of the women in the series.

Leighton-Lundberg was particularly interested in the way the fashion industry operates on masculine ideals (i.e. men dictating to women how they should dress). Writing in the 1990s, Leighton-Lundberg explained her conviction that the very idea of "fashion" is a masculine, stating: "I see women running around in these short skirts and long jackets and they can't even sit down. Why do they do that? They want to please."[123] In her mind, the fashions of the day were a chain, binding women into clothing created by men for the consumption of men rather than by and for the women themselves. Layered like swatches of fabric in a quilter's basket, the patterns within Leighton-Lundberg's paintings flicker and vibrate before the viewer's eyes. Colors

---

[120] Saleh, 30.
[121] Ibid. at 27.
[122] Sharon Gray, Interview by Rebekah Monahan. June 20, 2014.
[123] Ibid.

and shapes collide in an almost ferocious optical explosion. Because of this wildness, the women depicted within Leighton-Lundberg's paintings are imbued with a sense of independence and freedom. They are not held down by traditional rules of space, form, or appearance, nor are they subject to patriarchal rules on dress.

Leighton-Lundberg did not believe that women should dress for anyone other than themselves. She admired the approach of women who take control of their own "cultural form of dress rather than being told what women are supposed to wear." Leighton-Lundberg explained that the idea of the "sexy" woman is "pregnant with innuendo, [but] from another angle it's childlike."[124] Responding to the revealing nature of fashion in the male dominated industry, and perhaps also influenced by her conservative Mormon religion, Leighton-Lundberg's women appear in relatively modest, yet feminine gowns saturated with colorful patterns and floral designs. This is a gendered space of independence, a casting off of the rules of tradition, which interestingly, was the underlying premise of the Op-inspired Mod style prevalent during her young adult life.[125] Although she may not have been familiar with the terminology, Leighton-Lundberg was revealing the feminist concerns of commodification of women through fashion, self-objectification, the infantilization of women in her discussions of fashion and intersectionality.

With these concerns in mind, it isn't surprising that several of the ladies have had adjustments made to their necklines, although this is not consistent. Compare, for example, Matisse's *Woman with Oriental Dress* in *Entertaining Favorite Ladies III* (fig. 9) and the same figure in Entertaining Favorite Ladies: Millennial, or Bonnard's *Young Woman in the Garden* in *Entertaining Favorite Artists' Models* and again in *Entertaining Favorite Ladies II* (fig. 10). She has also veiled the back of Ingres' *Valpinçon Bather* in *Entertaining Favorite Ladies and Venus* and *Entertaining Favorite Ladies and Liberty* yet made no attempt to cover the rather voluptuous Gypsy Girl's chest from the Frans Hals painting by the same name. One thing that is consistent is the lack of nudity in the paintings. No matter the treatment of the original model (as virgin or prostitute), all the women that appear nude in the original have been dressed. The addition of clothing speaks to Leighton-Lundberg's interest in questioning the treatment of women as objects in art. Speaking of Manet's woman from *Luncheon on the Grass*, Leighton-Lundberg said, "[This] is the lady of Manet—the lady who sits naked in the park between two clothed gentlemen, which just scandalized Parisian society when it was painted. I always paint her with a dress on. When people see her they say to themselves, 'I know her, but I don't know from where,' and that's because I paint her with a dress on."[126]

---

[124] Ibid.
[125] The graphic, stylized patterns on the dresses worn by Leighton-Lundberg's ladies are similar to popular fashions from the 1960s—an interesting point, as many of graphic patterns which have come to define the trendy, hip look or "Mod" style of the era were themselves appropriated from Op art. Providing mixed reactions among Op artists, textile firms began producing Op fabric, which brought the style to runways and closets alike. Soon, Op patterns proliferated in pop culture, even coming to define the decade.
[126] Saleh, 30.

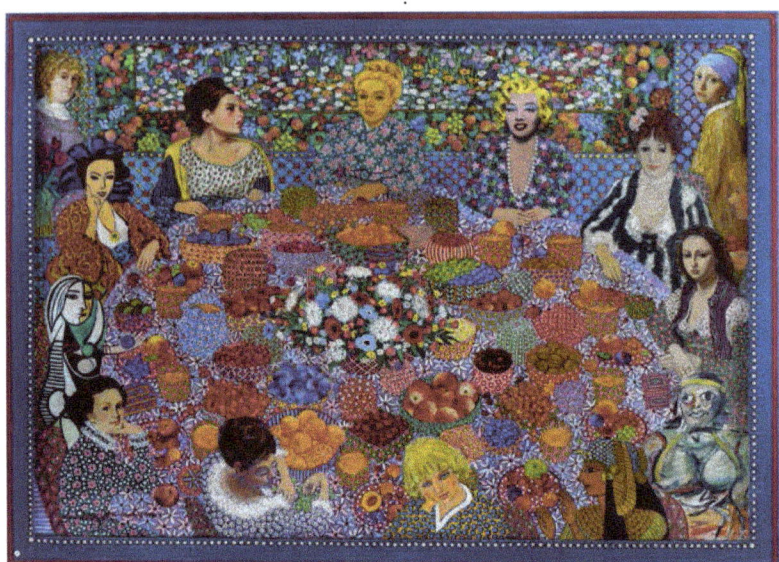

Fig. 10. Jeanne Leighton-Lundberg, *Entertaining: Favorite Ladies II*, 1992.
Springville Museum of Art (Springville, Utah).
Source: Courtesy the Jeanne Leighton-Lundberg Clarke Family Trust.

It isn't clear whether Leighton-Lundberg painted her in a dress to make her unrecognizable to viewers or if the lack of recognition is just an interesting consequence of the change in wardrobe. Thus, it is difficult to ascertain if Leighton-Lundberg modified the women's attire out of a sense of propriety, or if it was simply a way to present a unified composition. If instead Leighton-Lundberg had chosen to present the women dressed (or undressed) as they were in the originals, devoid of colorful patterns, the juxtaposition of so many figures in varying states of undress and artistic style would have caused a disjunction. The patterned clothing therefore acts as a secondary means of bringing the women to the same table. In this way, Leighton-Lundberg has altered the women to bring them closer together.

THE WOMEN (AND THEIR ARTISTS)

An analysis of the figures appearing in the "Favorite Ladies" paintings yields several interesting discoveries. First, the women were not chosen at random by Leighton-Lundberg or, in most cases, by popularity or renown of the paintings in which they appear. Instead, the women were chosen because they are in some way connected to their artist—as lovers, wives, daughters, or favorite models. It is believed that Vermeer modeled three of his subjects on his daughters (*Girl with a Flute, Girl in a Turban, Girl with a Red Hat*). Renoir's favorite model Nini Lopez, his wife Aline Charigot, and his children's nanny Gabrielle Renard are included, as are the wives of Modiglinani, Cézanne, and Matisse. Even Andy Warhol's pop art portrait of Liza

Minnelli reflects a connection, as the two were good friends. But while some are portraits of actual women others represent archetypes like Venus or the Odalisque.[127] The dichotomy between virgin and temptress, long examined by feminists, is an integral part of Leighton-Lundberg's work, and she recognizes that there is more to women than being either or: "I paint princesses and prostitutes and anything I happen to see that is appealing to me in terms of women."[128]

The second interesting discovery has to do with the number of times figures by a certain artist appear in the series. For example, the artists whose women appear most often are Picasso (nine figures in eight paintings), Degas (eight figures in seven paintings), and Manet (seven figures in seven paintings). Although Leighton-Lundberg once stated that she "never take[s] two women from the same painter in one painting,"[129] this is actually not true; two women from Picasso appear in the same painting as do two women from Degas. The fact that these three artists have paintings represented in almost every piece in the series speaks to the level of influence each had on Leighton-Lundberg's work.[130]

Interestingly, these three are also linked to one another through a chain of influence: Manet was the one who drew Degas into the Impressionist circle and is credited, in part, with turning Degas' attention to subjects of contemporary life such as café scenes and the ballet for which he is best known.[131] Degas' work was in turn inspiration for Picasso. According to Richard Kendall, "Degas was one of the artists Picasso never got out of his system. He gets into the ring with Degas, and then he retires slightly bruised, and then he gets back into the ring maybe another ten years later when something inspires him to rediscover Degas."[132] Over the course of a decade, Picasso created an entire series of paintings, prints, drawings based on the theme of a single Degas work, *In a Café (L'Absinthe)* (1875–1876).[133] Leighton-Lundberg may have been disaffected by their personalities, but there is no doubt she appreciated the contributions each made to art history and her inclusion of so many of their women perhaps also reveals an unconscious partiality for their work. Further analysis of these three masters makes this preference even more curious, considering her antipathy for sexism.

---

[127] Conjuring images of concubines and Middle Eastern harems, Odalisque refers to an eroticized genre of paintings "in which a nominally eastern woman lies on her side on display for the spectator," usually 19th century (French) male viewers. (Joan DelPlato, "Multiple Wives, Multiple Pleasures: Representing the Harem, 1800-1875." Fairleigh Dickenson University Press. 2002: 9.)

[128] Patricia Saleh, "A Feminist Symbolist." *Fine Art Collector International*. Vol. 2 No. 2 (1992): 29.

[129] Ibid.

[130] Leighton-Lundberg lists the following artists in her Master's Thesis as being most meaningful to her: Van Gogh, Matisse, Bonnard, Pollack, Johns, Vasarely, de Kooning, and Rothko. (Jeanne Lundberg Clarke, "A Considered Proposition of Reality: The Maximum Statement." Master's thesis, Brigham Young University, 1980.)

[131] Paul Trachtman, "Degas and His Dancers." *Smithsonian Magazine*. April 2003. Accessed November 4, 2016, https://www.smithsonianmag.com/arts-culture/degas-and-his-dancers-79455990/.

[132] Ann Landi, "Dancing with Degas." ARTNEWS. March 1, 2010. Accessed December 2014, http://www.artnews.com/2010/03/01/dancing-with-degas/.

[133] The exhibition "Picasso Looks at Degas" explored Picasso's 70-year obsession with Degas. It was displayed at the Sterling and Francine Clark Art Institute in Williamstown, Massachusetts in summer 2010 and then Museu Picasso in Barcelona in fall 2010.

Picasso: Gender Paradox

Leighton-Lundberg used women from Pablo Picasso's paintings in all eight works of the "Favorite Ladies" series. There are nine Picasso women in total, as two of his women appear together in *Favorite Ladies and a Little Delivery Boy*. Eight of the nine women are depictions of Marie-Thérèse Walter and Dora Maar, two of Picasso's great love interests. The ninth woman is his young daughter, Paloma (by mistress Françoise Gilot), from his 1950 painting *Claude et Paloma a joue*. As a feminist, Leighton-Lundberg's prolific use of Picasso is an interesting choice, when taking into account his views on and treatment of women.

In 1943, Picasso told his mistress 21-year-old Françoise Gilot (20 years his junior) at the onset of their nine-year affair that "women are machines for suffering."[134] He is also known for saying, "there are only two kinds of women—goddesses and doormats." Unfortunately for Gilot, the women whom Picasso initially viewed as goddesses would ultimately also become the doormats. An infamous womanizer, Picasso had affairs with dozens of women and was true to none of them.[135] According to writer and critic Mark Hudson, while many male artists draw obsessively from the faces and bodies of their wives and lovers, "no one used and abused his women quite like the greatest artist of the 20th century, Pablo Picasso."[136] Many times Leighton-Lundberg spoke of Picasso's negative perspective of women, fully aware of his passionate and brutal nature. Echoing Hudson's sentiments, Leighton-Lundberg said, "Picasso was not an enviable man, but his work was genius."[137]

The use of Marie-Thérèse Walter's and Dora Maar's images also speaks to Leighton-Lundberg's understanding of the importance these two women played during different periods of his life. Picasso drew and painted hundreds of portraits of his lovers, attempting to immortalize more than just how they looked, but the totality of his feelings toward them. This factor is important to Leighton-Lundberg's repeated inclusion of his women and relates directly to the question she hears the women in the "Favorite Ladies" series asking: "what do you think of the way he painted me?" Leighton-Lundberg believed the way Picasso painted women to be unflattering and "wretched,"[138] yet she still appreciated his great contributions to art.[139] Picasso's portraits of Walter and Maar are innovative and novel, even if they aren't particularly beautiful. She recognized that his portraits were more than a confusing jumble of facial features and body parts. Leighton-Lundberg probably appreciated that Picasso's women are not idealized versions of real people, but at the same time she had to have

---

[134] Annabel Venning, "How Picasso who called all women goddesses or doormats drove his lovers to despair and suicide." Dailymail. March 7, 2013, Accessed October 20, 2016. http://www.dailymail.co.uk/femail/article-2111329/How-Picasso-called-women-goddesses-doormats-drove-lovers-despair-suicide-cruelty-betrayal.html#ixzz37aIPowEA

[135] "Pablo Picasso's love affair with women." *The Telegraph*. February 13, 2009. Accessed October 15, 2016, http://www.telegraph.co.uk/culture/art/4610752/Pablo-Picassos-love-affair-with-women.html.

[136] Ibid.

[137] Saleh, 30.

[138] Ibid.

[139] Matthew Clarke, Interview by Rebekah Monahan. November 9, 2013.

seen them as objectifications—women as Picasso sees them. And for Leighton-Lundberg, that was likely quite complicated. After all, she admired his work but not his person.

Interestingly, much of Picasso's work represents a dialogue with the great masters of European art (including Velázquez, Goya, Rembrandt, Delacroix, Ingres, Degas, Manet and Cézanne) as he explored the artistic concerns of the past and made "audacious responses" to their work.[140] He repeatedly went back to the grand traditions of Western art as his own style developed and this is obvious in the traditional subjects of still lifes, self-portraits, the female nude, and seated females figures present in his work. Picasso became one of the most—if not the most—influential artist of the 20th century. The "genius" Leighton-Lundberg spoke of is obvious in his innovative style and complexity of composition. His interest in the masters of old is echoed in Leighton-Lundberg's work as she also concerns herself with the history of those artists who came before her. Leighton-Lundberg was surely following in their footsteps. Once again, it becomes clear that Leighton-Lundberg's incorporation of the women from his paintings rather than a self-portrait of the artist is a way to recognize his artistic contributions without recognizing the artist directly.[141]

DEGAS: BEAUTY AND THE MISOGYNIST

Two ballerinas, a milliner, an opera singer, and a prostitute—what sounds like the beginning of a bad joke is actually a list of the Degas figures represented in Leighton-Lundberg's "Favorite Ladies" paintings. The second most repeated artist in the series, Edgar Degas's women appear eight times in seven paintings (with the ballerinas and milliner each appearing twice). While none of Degas' women are included in one work in the series, *Entertaining Favorite Ladies and Venus*, she appears in two forms in *Entertaining Favorite Ladies and Liberty*, first as *The Opera Singer Performs* (1876) and second as *Women on a Café Terrace in the Evening* (1877). An important, easily recognizable figure in modern art, Degas seems a straightforward choice to be so well represented in Leighton-Lundberg's work. However, like Picasso, the closer one looks, the more interesting her selection of him becomes.

A founder and leading member of the Impressionist movement,[142] Degas' major contributions to art history include experimentation with a variety of media, reviving the use of pastels, incorporating photograph-like elements in his work through the use of unusual vantage points, cropping compositions and cutting off figures, and the use of asymmetrical framing, and of course, his choice of subject: modern, working class women such as dancers, prostitutes, laundresses, and other "denizens of Parisian low

---

[140] "Picasso: Challenging the Past." National Gallery of Art. Accessed June 8, 2015, http://www.nationalgallery.org.uk/whats-on/past/picasso-challenging-the-past.

[141] Jeanne did name one of her many cats "Picasso." And although Picasso the cat met a rather fateful end, she buried him in a place of honor in her garden on the hill.

[142] Edgar Degas seems never to have reconciled himself to the label of "Impressionist," preferring to call himself a "Realist" or "Independent." Nevertheless, he was one of the group's founders, an organizer of its exhibitions, and one of its most important core members.

life."¹⁴³ Thus, a clear choice for Leighton-Lundberg, as her work reflects several of these elements. Ultimately, Degas is responsible for some of the most popular images of nineteenth-century art.

While Leighton-Lundberg's "Favorite Ladies" compositions uphold traditional symmetry, she does incorporate cropping, and the use of an unusual combination point of view (which is especially obvious in the "Family Life" series). Unlike Degas, her paintings lack literal depth, with very little change in the size of figures from front to back, and a very flat table in the middle. While the "ladies" are cut in the way they appear in their original paintings, Leighton-Lundberg incorporates a snapshot feel by adding other characters of her own design to frame the lower edge. Of these characters, only hands and the backs of heads are visible (see, for example, *Entertaining Favorite Ladies I*, fig. 11).

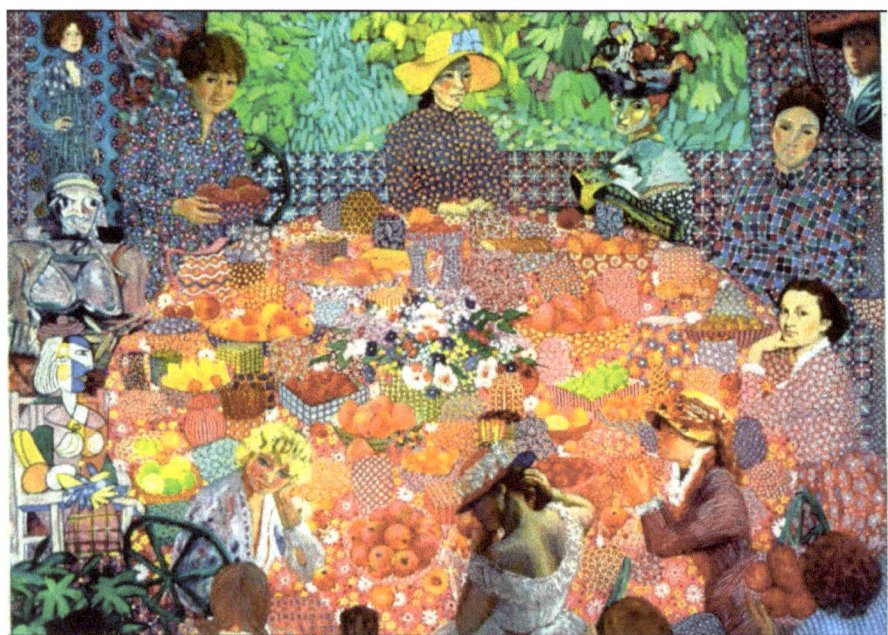

Fig. 11. Jeanne Leighton-Lundberg, *Favorite Ladies I*, c. 1987. Jeanne Leighton-Lundberg Clarke Family Trust.
Source: Courtesy the Jeanne Leighton-Lundberg Clarke Family Trust.

Degas' subject matter is also interesting in the discussion of how it influenced Leighton-Lundberg's work. Within Degas' robust repertoire of work are included dozens of images of laundresses and milliners, and approximately 1,500 works on the

---

¹⁴³ Ruth Schenkel, "Edgar Degas (1834-1917): Painting and Drawing." Heilbrunn Timeline of Art History. The Metropolitan Museum of Art. October 2004. Accessed October 15, 2016, https://www.metmuseum.org/toah/hd/dgsp/hd_dgsp.htm.

subject of ballet.[144] Degas was, according to art historian Elizabeth Cowling, "utterly obsessed with women and their lives."[145] The same could be said for Leighton-Lundberg, who rarely painted men, and (as quoted above) painted any and all types of women she found appealing. With the exception of her still lifes, the sole subject matter of her works is women and their lives. Degas' obsession with women has been linked to Picasso's, but while this obsession with women translated from Picasso's work to his multiple marriages and love affairs, Degas' love life was more turbid. According to Cowling, "there are small references in his papers which tell us that in fact he did have some sexual contact, probably with prostitutes and models. There was never a lover, though, whose name has come down to us."[146] While his love life remains a mystery, what has been well documented is Degas' misogyny.

During the 1980s to 1990s, as Leighton-Lundberg was painting this series, a lively discussion of Degas and his works took place in the art history community.[147] The discussion revolved around not talking about Degas, a sort of revisionist mission, predicated on Degas' misogyny, which ultimately kept everyone talking about Degas. Why was he obsessively fixated by the female nude, and bathers in particular? Were his voyeuristically styled paintings evidence of perversion? And if so, should Degas, personally or artistically, be removed from the canon of art history? With the wave of these art historians' pens, could he magically be considered no longer relevant?

Out of historical context, Degas' paintings of ballerinas stretching and dancing appear to be beautiful representations of a romantic occupation. But in reality, the vibrant colors only serve as an initial mask for the harsh realities of the nineteenth-century dancers' lives. The golden age of the Parisian ballet long since over, ballet during the time Degas painted it was no longer a performance "art" to which fine folk flocked, but rather a somewhat scandalous interlude for operas, as the ballerinas danced in tights and leotards, revealing attire for the Victorian era.[148] Besides being leered at by bored operagoers, many of the ballerinas came from poor families and were paid so little they had to resort to prostitution in order to meet ends meet.[149] The dance itself was a grueling and physically arduous sport. Many ballerinas were forced to dance in corsets, dangerously restricting their ability to breathe.

Degas was fascinated by the pain endured by the dancers and was himself cruel to his models. As his eyesight began to fade, he hired ballerinas to model for him in his studio, sometimes obliging them "to pose for hours on end—legs extended or bent, arms held high overhead—in excruciating discomfort, even for dancers inured to pain."[150] In his later life Degas commented that, "I have perhaps too often considered women as an animal." Speaking of his work, and the paintings of bathers in particular,

---

[144] Ibid.
[145] Ann Landi, "Dancing with Degas." ARTNEWS. March 1, 2010. Accessed December 2014, http://www.artnews.com/2010/03/01/dancing-with-degas/.
[146] Ibid.
[147] Norma Broude, "Review of "Dealing with Degas: Representations of Women and the Politics of Vision" by Richard Kendall and Griselda Pollock." *Women's Art Journal*. Vol. 16, No. 2.
[148] John Richardson, "Degas and the Dancers." Vanity Fair. October 2002. Accessed October 15, 2016, http://www.vanityfair.com/news/2002/10/degas200210.
[149] Ibid.
[150] Ibid.

he said later in life, "Women can never forgive me; they hate me, they can feel that I am disarming them. I show them without their coquetry, in the state of animals cleaning themselves."[151]

This is an interesting contrast to the way Leighton-Lundberg presents her women, but also speaks to her grand question. Did the "depressingly dog-faced bunch" of ballerinas (photographs confirm the majority of ballerinas did not meet conventional standards of nineteenth-century beauty)[152] appear to Leighton-Lundberg as having been unfairly or cruelly represented?[153] Or did she see within the images of sharply angled arms, arching backs, over-stretched, and overworked bodies realistic depictions of strong, able women doing the best they could with what they were given, rather than a cruel, misogynist, animalistic view of women? As Norma Broude, a foremost scholar on Degas, has pointed out, not all images of women in male art should be characterized as sexist. Broude's 1975 paper explains that "the description of Degas as 'misogynist' by his art critic contemporaries resulted from their own sex-biased expectations, founded in masculine concepts of conventional female beauty which blinded the writers (and later art historians) to Degas' atypically sympathetic images of women as independent and sometimes vibrantly intellectual figures."[154] While this doesn't excuse the treatment of his models, it does give an alternative explanation for his indifference toward graceful idealization, and why it was interpreted as hatred rather than realism: Degas' images of women posed a threat and challenge to "those more idealized images that were conventionally used in the 19th century to mask the subordination, commodification, and exploitation of women in Western society." [155]

Leighton-Lundberg's inclusion of eight of Degas working women speaks to her belief that there continues to be a place for Degas' work in art history and society, despite his perceived beliefs and feelings toward women. She had literally hundreds of Degas paintings to pull from, yet she chose ones of women with their arms raised at sharp angles, their faces in profile or partially obscured by shadow—not seated portraits, but images of labor. Rather than trying to dismantle the construct of Degas, Leighton-Lundberg gives the women a new opportunity to commune with viewers outside the confines of a stage, milliners shop, or café. Do they look tired, pained, or overworked? It may just be, in Leighton-Lundberg's experience, because they were.

MANET AND THE ABSURDITY OF THE TRADITIONAL NUDE

Édouard Manet's woman from *Luncheon on the Grass* (*Le déjeuner sur l'herbe*) (1862–1863) appears in seven of the eight paintings in the "Favorite Ladies" series.

---

[151] Ibid.

[152] Paul Trachtman, "Degas and His Dancers." Smithsonian Magazine. April 2003. Accessed November 4, 2016 < https://www.smithsonianmag.com/arts-culture/degas-and-his-dancers-79455990/>

[153] In a sonnet written c. 1889, Degas addressed the ballerinas with this quip: "Queens are made of distance and greasepaint."

[154] Norma Broude and Mary D. Garrard, "Feminist Art History and the Academy: Where Are We Now?," Women's Studies Quarterly 25, No. 1/2 (1997), 214.

[155] Ibid.

This painting gained critical attention under the title "Le Bain" at the first Salon des Refusés after being rejected from the 1863 Paris Salon.[156] Leighton-Lundberg's inclusion of this particular painting is significant for two reasons. First, Manet pulled from two classical paintings in creating *Luncheon on the Grass*. The arrangement of the figures was taken from Raphael's *Judgment of Paris* (1520) and the subject matter is a tribute to Titian's *Concert Champêtre* (c. 1509). Leighton-Lundberg's "Favorite Ladies" paintings also pull from recognizable, traditional paintings. Second—and this was the main reason why the painting became the primary attraction at the 1863 Salon des Refusés—Manet's composition forces the viewer to admit the absurdity of the traditional nude, thereby questioning the treatment of women in art, a similar question to that which Leighton-Lundberg asks in the "Favorite Ladies" series.

Both Raphael's and Titian's works are examples of classical treatment of the female nude: she sits disrobed, in an idyllic landscape, surrounded by clothed men. But unlike the classical works that inspired them, Manet's women are not Roman goddesses or Greek nymphs. Instead, they are French women and more importantly, modern French women. Having discarded her clothing, the woman is not "nude" but naked, sitting unabashed in the company of two equally modern—yet fully clothed—gentlemen. The naked woman confronts the audience with a direct gaze unlike most classical nudes, which glance off to the side allowing viewers to look at their bodies uninterrupted. Thus, Manet's painting, like Leighton-Lundberg's "Favorite Ladies," also questions the treatment of women as objects in paintings in art history. Is the woman object or subject? Her confrontational yet bemused look suggest that she is the voice asking for a reconsideration of all nudes that came before her. It is also important to note that the figures in the painting are Victorine Meurent, a favorite model of the artist, Manet's brother-in-law Ferdinand Leenhoff, and his younger brother Eugene.[157] The fact that the sitters were recognizable as real individuals rather than anonymous muses was also an affront to viewers at the time. Taken together, and setting aside any potential allusion to prostitution, these elements made for a nonsensical composition in a contemporary nineteenth-century context. In every way possible Manet was pushing at social norms.

Clearly Manet's work is a direct influence on Leighton-Lundberg's "Favorite Ladies" thesis. The inclusion of this woman in all but one of the eight works lends credence to the fact that she was inspired by the work in more ways than one. It is interesting to consider the implications of her appearing in a dress. As mentioned above, it makes it hard for viewers to identify her as belonging to the painting, but at the same time it brings attention to her as a person rather than the focus of a scandalous work of art by a garish artist.

---

[156] "Edouard Manet Luncheon on the Grass." Musée D'Orsay: Works in Focus. 2006. Musée D'Orsay. Accessed August 1, 2014. http://www.museeorsay.fr/index.php?id=851&L=1&tx_commentaire_pi1[showUid]=7123.

[157] "Reinterpreted Artworks: Le Déjeuner sur l'Herbe by Edouard Manet." New Britain Museum of American Art. April 27, 2010. https://nbmaa.wordpress.com/2010/04/27/reinterpreted-artworks-le-dejeuner-sur-l%E2%80%99herbe-by-edouard-manet/

No Women Artists?

After looking at these three artists, and keeping in mind that all 25 of the identified ladies' artists are male, the question that has to be asked is why didn't Leighton-Lundberg include images of women by women artists? Is it because she wasn't influenced by their work or didn't consider them as competent or innovative or interesting? This seems unlikely. True, the textbooks of the day consistently excluded the contributions of women artists, and yes, in the canon of art history those considered "great artists" are largely (white) men,[158] but it is doubtful that a women as extensively read and well educated as Leighton-Lundberg would not have been familiar with the contributions of Artemisia Gentileschi (1593-c. 1656), Angelica Kauffman (1741-1807), Mary Cassatt (1844-1926), Frida Kahlo (1907-1954), or Georgia O'Keefe (1887-1986) to name a few.[159] Not to mention her contemporaries Judy Chicago (1939-) and Mary Beth Edelson (1933-). No, it is more likely that Leighton-Lundberg excluded female artists because the purpose behind the series was to answer the question "how have women been represented by men artists throughout art history?" Remember that Leighton-Lundberg's thesis (maximalism) seeks to represent a woman's experience, and in the case of the "Favorite Ladies," the experiences of artists' models. So perhaps Leighton-Lundberg didn't include Mary Cassatt because she didn't feel it necessary to question the legitimacy of how she, a fellow woman artist, represented a woman's experience in her art. Although conjecture, this lends credence to the idea that Leighton-Lundberg's thesis rests on the premise that women cannot be sexist or misogynist, an unfortunate assumption considering the representations of women by women artists aligned with the Cult of True Womanhood. However, one cannot necessarily fault Leighton-Lundberg for having a narrowly focused thesis, and as such, we will return to the discussion of the "Favorite Ladies" series.

Comparison to Contemporary Feminist Artists

Of her dining paintings, Leighton-Lundberg once explained, "I paint myself, literally. And my women paintings include a profile of myself serving the other women at the table who come from all different centuries and cultures. They all get together at my

---

[158] Gemma Rolls-Bentley's survey of the 2012 top 100 auction sales ranked by price found that not a single one was female (highly valued meaning considered "great" or "genius").
Kira Cochrane, "Women in art: why are all the 'great' artists men?" *The Guardian.* May 24, 2013. Accessed March 15, 2015. https://www.theguardian.com/lifeandstyle/the-womens-blog-with-jane-martinson/2013/may/24/women-art-great-artists-men.

[159] "I knew I was taking a position that directly contradicted my stance in "Why Have There Been No Great Women Artists?" Yet it seemed to me that, after digging around in the basements and reserves of great European museums and provincial art galleries, there had indeed been many wonderfully inventive, extremely competent, and above all, unquestionably interesting woman artists; some of these artists had been cherished and admired on their own native turf, even if they could not be considered so-called international superstars." Linda Nochlin, "Starting from Scratch: The Beginnings of Feminist Art History," in *The Power of Feminist Art: The American Movement of the 1970s, History and Impact*, eds. Norma Broude and Mary D. Garrard, (New York: H.N. Abrams, 1994), 137.

table and talk life over."[160] To anyone familiar with twentieth century art, the concept of an all-female dinner party immediately conjures comparisons to the legendary Judy Chicago, whose *Dinner Party* (1974-79) is the stuff of feminist legend, and Mary Beth Edelson's *Some Living American Woman Artists/Last Supper*, also an important icon of 1970s feminist art.

Chicago's infamous multimedia work, now on display at the Brooklyn Museum of Art, features an enormous triangular table (the arms are 48 feet long), bedecked with 39 individualized place settings, each dedicated to a specific woman from history, from the Primordial Goddess to Ishtar, Sacajawea, and Georgia O'Keeffe. Inscribed in gold on the tile floor beneath the table are 999 additional names of significant women.[161]

An elaborate project that took six years and hundreds of volunteers to complete, *The Dinner Party* provoked a conservative backlash when it was unveiled, even being labeled as "pornographic" due to the artist's use of butterfly/vaginal imagery in the designs of the place settings. These accusations seem almost ludicrous today, considering the abstract nature of the shapes, and the fact that one of Chicago's intentions was to honor the great women of the past, many of whom had been lost to history. But she was working in the late 1970s, a time when historical images of female nudity, eroticism, and even violence were common subjects in museums and textbooks but works created by women were almost never included in the canon of art history, no matter the subject, style, or quality.

Mary Beth Edelson's poster *Some Living American Woman Artists/Last Supper* (1971) features a reproduction of Leonardo da Vinci's *Last Supper* (1495–1498) with the heads of woman artists superimposed over the figures who are, of course, Christ and his disciples. Appropriating Western masterpieces in this manner was, "a typical strategy of feminist artists, who wished to expose the ways that the traditions of art have used the image of Woman, without granting real women their place within the profession."[162]

Edelson and Chicago were motivated by the "programmatic cultural and historical exclusion"[163] of women artists from the dialogue of art history obvious in the omission of women artists from popular art history textbooks of the 1960s and 1970s. Even in 1979, when asked why his influential textbook, *History of Art,* did not include the name of a single woman artist, author H. W. Janson replied, "I have not been able to find a woman artist who clearly belongs in a one-volume history of art."[164] Leighton-Lundberg was studying art at exactly this time. She would have studied from textbooks that did not include women artists. Indeed, Chicago once

---

[160] Saleh, 29.
[161] "Exhibitions: The Dinner Party by Judy Chicago." Brooklyn Museum. Accessed June 8, 2015, http://www.brooklynmuseum.org/exhibitions/dinner_party/
[162] Linda S. Aleci, "In a Pig's Eye: The Offence of Some Living American Women Artists." Mary Beth Edelson. Accessed June 8, 2015, http://www.marybethedelson.com/essay_pigeye.html.
[163] Ibid.
[164] Broude, Norma, Mary D. Garrard, and Judith K. Brodsky. *The Power of Feminist Art: The American Movement of the 1970s, History and Impact.* (New York: H.N. Abrams, 1994), 16. The current edition of the book is not much more inclusive: only 27 women are represented.

stated, "Because we are denied knowledge of our history, we are deprived of standing upon each other's shoulders and building upon each other's hard-earned accomplishments. Instead, we are condemned to repeat what others have done before us and thus we continually reinvent the wheel."[165]

Leighton-Lundberg also embraced a feminist artistic approach, but not the radical feminism characteristic of New York artists and the Women's Liberation movement. Leighton-Lundberg was more aligned with the West Coast feminists, like Judy Chicago and Miriam Shapiro, who sought to raise awareness of gender and womanhood, even celebrating the feminine and all of its tangential qualities. Leighton-Lundberg's dining scenes share this interest in gender and identity in two ways. Firstly, Leighton-Lundberg elevates the concept of the female community. Her dinner parties are meetings points for women of different centuries and cultures-- places where women can talk freely of their lives, their experiences, and their struggles. Indeed, Leighton-Lundberg did not shy away from the use of "gendered" objects like flowers and fruit. The spaces presented in her paintings are also of the traditionally feminine kind: kitchens, dining rooms, and other home settings decorated in rich patterns that exude femininity. She said, "Our lives as women are complex. We are jugglers, trying to be mothers, career women, lovers, housekeepers—the overextended all-around handywoman. We pray that our humor holds up, and that time allows us some pleasures and some freedom to express ourselves. A minimalist art certainly cannot symbolize a woman's experience"[166] Thus, Leighton-Lundberg understood that women's lives take many forms and her paintings reflect that aspect of feminism, arguing for maximalism to be taken seriously.

Secondly, Leighton-Lundberg, like Chicago, united past and present in her paintings by turning to historical sources. While it is uncertain whether Leighton-Lundberg was aware of Edelson's and Chicago's work, it seems likely. Nevertheless, Leighton-Lundberg's work is not derivative. That all three use a table is curious considering the domestic implications it entails, yet all three present the situation as women being served rather than serving. However, Leighton-Lundberg's use of the table is arguably more meaningful because she has involved the women directly rather than setting them an empty place or using only their heads. Rather than a substitution or name card, Leighton-Lundberg's women are present and driving. While all three artists present similar ideas, the actual concepts are formed in a markedly different manner. Educated and well-read in the history of art, there is no doubt that Leighton-Lundberg was similarly motivated to question the way women have been concurrently omitted as participants in art history and objectified as the silent subjects of male artists. But while Edelson and Chicago focused on creating art that brought women artists to the table of history,[167] Leighton-Lundberg used the table to question the way women have been represented by male artists, as objects of the male gaze rather than subjects in their own right.

---

[165] Alvis Clendenen, *Experiencing Hildegard: Jungian Perspectives* (Wilmette, Ill.: Chiron Publications, 2009), 31.
[166] Carol Lea Clark, "Jeanne Leighton-Lundberg," *Southwest Art Magazine* (October 1989): 87.
[167] Broude, Garrard, and Brodsky, 16.

FAVORITE LADIES CONCLUSION

Appropriated from the work of artists such as Vermeer, Manet, Degas, Picasso, and de Kooning, Leighton-Lundberg's whimsical dinner parties of interesting figures, both historical and fictional, are transformed from the objects of male desire into psychological, emotional, and intellectual beings. She imbued them with personality, begging us as viewers to wonder, what would these women say if they could speak? We have looked at their faces for hundreds of years, and have accepted them as beautiful objects, but what if we look below the surface of their pretty faces? Such was the transformation of the female psyche during the 1970s. In discussing her view on women in history, Leighton-Lundberg drew parallels to female plight: "Some women have had to sustain themselves and their families because men were unfaithful to them and have run off. So, women have had to become stronger, and that story is not over yet. It is just the beginning."[168]

In the same way that women are too complicated for Minimalism to represent their existence, Leighton-Lundberg believed that she was too complicated to be fitted with labels like "female artist." According to Leighton-Lundberg's longtime friend and colleague, Sharon Gray, "[Sometimes] she would get on her soapbox about 'I am not a feminist, they don't represent me.' But, at other times she was okay with it. There really was no question that she was a feminist, just whether or not she would call herself that."[169] This sentiment was shared by many woman[170] of Leighton-Lundberg's generation who had struggled for a long time to reconcile the identities of "female" and "artist." She didn't want to be confined by labels like feminist or Mormon or female. She was very comfortable with her own views and opinions and she knew her style. Leighton-Lundberg didn't feel that being any of these things (female, Mormon, feminist) was negative or limited her abilities in terms of painting, but she didn't want others to limit their response to her work (or disregard it altogether) because of those labels. In the same way, Leighton-Lundberg used the "Favorite Ladies" series to free these particular models, mistresses, princesses, and prostitutes from the stereotypes and caricatures assigned to them by challenging the way all women have been represented and labeled in art history.

Thus, when Leighton-Lundberg used pattern formally and symbolically in her paintings, she was purposefully calling to mind traditional women's work like quilting and embroidery. By refusing to be boxed in by labels, she too sought to challenge the notion of what was "women's art." While some women artists tried to fight labels by producing art that would align them with the Minimalist boy's club, Leighton-Lundberg embraced her artistic calling and owned her style of maximalist art in an inclusive and humanizing manner. To her it was not "women's" art but simply art.

---

[168] Saleh, 30.
[169] Sharon Gray. Interview by Rebekah Monahan. June 20, 2014.
[170] American art historian Linda Nochlin said, "I have always been a feminist, albeit a partly unconscious and often confused one." (Broude and Garrard, The Power of Feminist Art, 132).

Maximalism and Visual Delight

CHAPTER 5

The Maximalist Legacy

Jeanne Leighton-Lundberg was a maximalist pioneer. She appropriated from the modernist past to create a wholly postmodern approach to contemporary genre painting. Ahead of her time, Leighton-Lundberg tapped into a decorative spirit that would gain momentum in the new millennium. Although the term maximalism is most commonly used as a tag or description rather than as a formalized stylistic approach, maximalist methods have witnessed a recent upsurge in contemporary art and design. This concluding chapter expands and informs the developing dialogue of Maximalism in the early twenty-first century by providing resources on maximalist trends and themes, including maximalism and visual rebellion, maximalist design, and maximal cultural messages.

ANYTHING AND EVERYTHING: MAXIMAL EXPERIENCE AND VISUAL REBELLION

Perhaps because maximalism is typically described as the antithesis of minimalism, maximal artists are often regarded as rebels and rule-breakers, countering a system of methods, maxims, and hierarchies. They seemingly throw the rulebook out of the metaphorical window in order to explore new territory. Contemporary artist Takashi Murakami, whose work is associated with the maximalist tag, has underscored the explorative, radical nature of maximalism by paralleling it with the conservative nature of minimalism: "The concept of minimalism is to relax. Like a Zen monk in training, it is something that brings equilibrium to the heart."[171] Whereas, maximalism represents the opposite: "I have never traveled to outer space and have thus never felt the fearsome limitlessness of that pitch-black world, but I think that perhaps this is the true maximalism that we are discussing here."[172]

Thus, maximalism is understood as being mysterious, uncharted, and limitless. It is emptiness and fullness, anything and everything. In literature, maximalist works are long and complex, employing abundant literary devices and techniques, such as David Foster Wallace's acclaimed Infinite Jest, categorized as an encyclopedia novel with numerous digressions and an intricate web of endnotes.[173] In contemporary music, maximalism is often associated with works that push the limits of the listener via

---

[171] Takashi Murakami, "Why More Is More." Esquire. August 17, 2008. http://www.esquire.com/style/a4917/takashi-murakami-0908/
[172] Ibid.
[173] For more information, see: Stefano Ercolino, The Maximalist Novel: From Thomas Pynchon's Gravity's Rainbow to Roberto Bolano's 2666 (New York: Bloomsbury Academic, 2015).

vocals, acoustics, emotional content, or sheer volume.[174] American composer Milton Babbitt has been associated with maximalism, as well as Frank Zappa, and Kanye West. In his review of Michel Delville's, *Frank Zappa, Captain Beefheart and the Secret History of Maximalism* (2005), Martin Knakkergaard asserted, "Maximalism is presented as a specific genre or existential modality more or less defined by its limitlessness: anything can be seen as or turned into an expressive means of the artist, and the boundaries between what belongs to the aesthetics and what does not are fluctuating, if they exist at all."[175] In the realm of film, Baz Luhrmann (*Romeo + Juliet, The Great Gatsby*) and Wes Anderson (*The Grand Budapest Hotel, Life Aquatic*) are surely maximalist directors, although maximalism is not a term often coupled with cinema. This might be due, however, to the proliferation of contemporary films that already embrace the maximalist spirit (maximal effects have come to be expected in the film industry).

Maximalists are often visionaries, rebelling against the status quo to produce work that strives to be unique and experimental. As a Young British Artist, Damien Hirst exhibited strong maximalist tendencies, as evidenced by his kaleidoscope murals composed of thousands of butterfly wings, as well as his black mural/assemblages created of thousands of dead flies. Brazilian photographer and sculptor Vic Muniz has employed maximal principles with his large-scale assemblage works that focus on social injustice, such as "Pictures of Garbage," a series created during Muniz's travels to Rio de Janeiro to collaborate with garbage pickers in the world's largest landfill. For this series, Muniz used trash to re-create historical works of art, such as Jacques Louis David's *Death of Marat* (1793), creating large-scale assemblage works to be photographed. Takashi Murakami, as referenced above, embraces maximalism in his signature Superflat style, which combines anime, manga, and fine art. Borrowing from comics, graphic design, and consumer culture, Murakami's vivid, pop-hued paintings embrace the spirit of assemblage in their overlay of imagery, logos, and designs.

Assemblage, whether visual or conceptual, is a cornerstone of maximalist approaches, complimenting the "anything and everything" nature of the movement and cutting across techniques, mediums, and categories of art. The assemblage method reflects the rebellious, and sometimes precocious, nature of maximalist work, which questions the hegemony of balance, order, and structure, instead celebrating excess, decorative overload, visual minutiae, and controlled chaos. Despite the lack of conformity to a single aesthetic, one characteristic is present in almost every artwork described as maximal: the juxtaposition of Part vs. Whole. Visual overload cannot be created without surplus. Whether two- or three-dimensional in form, all maximal works are assemblages. Although, rather than endeavoring to create a seamlessly unified whole, maximalists focus on individual parts. Gestalt is not a guiding principle. Hierarchy is restructured through extravagant layering and repetition. Shapes, patterns, colors, and imagery compete for attention. Backgrounds are no

---

[174] The term "Aristocratic Maximalism" has been used in reference to ballet from sixteenth-century France to nineteenth-century Russia.
[175] Knakkergaard, 328.

longer backdrops; focal points multiply, teasing the eye in a visual banter. Jeanne Leighton-Lundberg's "Favorite Ladies" series illustrates this point well: the ring of ladies surrounding the banquet table in each painting competes visually with the patterning on the table itself. Subdividing further, each portrait could easily detach from the composition to form a separate, independent work.

Taking a step backward, deconstructive-reconstructive impulses were a guiding force throughout the modernist era as apparent in such styles as Cubism, Futurism, Dada, Surrealism, and Pop. Artists explored the interaction of Part vs. Whole through such techniques as collage, photomontage, and assemblage. From Pablo Picasso and Georges Braque's first experimentations with papier collé to Kurt Schwitters' "Merz pictures" and Louise Nevelson's wood collages, the potential of mixed media revolutionized the concept of composition. Whether through appropriations, readymades, montages, or assemblages, artists could isolate, select, and reconstruct. Readymade content, be it in the form of cut paper, detritus, or recycled content, allowed artists to experiment with shape, form, and composition typically employing hard-edged lines and sharply defined shapes.

These same approaches also presented rich opportunities for visual excess. For example, Kurt Schwitters incorporated actual trash in his collages, such as *Merz Picture 32 A, The Cherry Picture* (1921), an amalgam of cut-and-pasted colored and printed-paper with cloth, wood, metal, and cork, as well as overlaid oil, pencil, and ink. Bridging Dadaism, Constructivism, assemblage, and graphic design, the work presents the viewer with a proliferation of disconnected components to piece through: candy wrappers, newspaper clippings, images of cherries and kittens, even a broken pipe. Louise Nevelson would also draw compositions from detritus, although she would focus on wooden objects (like chair legs and balusters) that she would arrange in compartmentalized, mural-sized installations, such as *An American Tribute to the British People* (1960-64). Although painted in solid, unifying colors (such as black, white, or gold) Nevelson's large-scale accumulations present the viewer with a maximalist approach to form and detail.

Painters were likewise impacted by the additive qualities of assemblage and collage-based techniques. Mid-century American modernist Stuart Davis, for example, embraced the look of papier collé in his vividly hued urban landscapes and interior scenes. The almost electrified *Swing Landscape* of 1938 reveals Stuart's fascination with the Jazz Age, manifested through bold, contrasting colors that vibrate across the surface of the canvas as well as rhythmic, sharp-edged forms that look like flat shapes cut from paper. *The Mellow Pad* (1945-51), a modernist approach to genre painting, similarly creates a visual explosion of hard-edged confetti colors punctuated by dynamic black shapes that compete to be noticed. Foreground and background fold together, creating maximal surface design of patterns, boxes, circles, and Miro-esque organic shapes.

The reconstructive nature of maximalist paintings can lend to visual fragmentation: artworks nest within artworks, like a type of artistic microcosm. Although incorporating a primarily blue and orange color palette, Jeanne Leighton-Lundberg's *Family in Blue* (fig. 2) exemplifies the nesting quality of maximalist works: the table, adorned in a turquoise blue checkerboard tablecloth, dominates the picture plane, ornamented with a scattering of dishes, bowls, and mounds of food that could form individual still life paintings. *Family in Blue* contains three distinct components: the table itself (with mother and child on the periphery) occupying the bottom two-thirds of the work, the father in blue standing against patterned blue wallpaper in the upper left quadrant, and, in the upper right quadrant, the opening into an adjacent tangerine-hued room where a boy practices piano. Each of these components creates paintings within the painting, which could be subdivided again and again (the basket of plums on the table, for example, could form a detached still life painting).

Because of their decadent excess, maximal works do not typically emphasize unity and balance. Individual parts do not always merge into a seamless whole. These characteristics sharply contrast with the minimalist aesthetic, which focused primarily on the whole. The work of Piet Mondrian provides an ideal counterpoint to the maximalist aesthetic: "One feels, when looking at a Mondrian, that it is the attunement of the whole which is the only real value, indeed, the only real thing or quality in the painting," historian Daniel Herwitz has noted of the Neoplasticist. "One feels that without the whole the parts would disintegrate entirely into a kind of nothingness, that without the whole the parts would have neither meaning, integrity, nor identity."[176] The same would not be said of maximalism.

Maximalists embrace the power of deconstructive/reconstructive techniques not to produce a unified gestalt wherein the whole is greater than the sum of its parts, but to emphasize the visual contribution of each component within a "more is more" aesthetic. The proliferation of individual parts assists in the achievement of maximal results. This continual push and pull between Part and Whole also reflects the polarized nature of maximalism, which is often couched in binary terms: maximal/minimal, decorative/ascetic, complex/simple, full/empty. Thus, maximalism provides an alternative to (or escape from) the modernist and academic traditions by inviting viewers to experience, in the words of Takashi Murakami, fearsome limitlessness. But this is not constrained to painting and sculpture. Recent years have witnessed a marked upsurge in experimentation with maximalist design from graphic design and interior design, to fashion, architecture, and even branding.

MORE IS MORE: MAXIMALIST DESIGN AND VISUAL OVERLOAD

While maximalist impulses can be seen throughout the history of art and intermittently during the past century, recent years have observed a newfound fascination with maximalist approaches to design in all forms. In January 2017, the Wall Street Journal published, "Maximalism: The Lush New Décor Look That's Vanquishing Minimalism."[177] During the same year, The New York Times,

---

[176] Daniel Herwitz, *Making Theory/Constructing Art: On the Authority of the Avant-Garde* (Chicago: University of Chicago Press, 1996): 105-106.
[177] Julie Lasky, "Maximalism: The Lush New Décor Look That's Vanquishing Minimalism." *The Wall Street Journal*, January 26, 2017. https://www.wsj.com/articles/the-lush-new-decor-look-thats-vanquishing-minimalism-1485463384

proclaimed: "The Maximalists Are Coming,"[178] while the Architect's Newspaper posed the question, "Why is Maximalism Taking Over the World?"[179] Before addressing the question of why, let us focus on the matter of how. Since the turn of the twenty-first century, and increasing during the past ten years, maximalism has been gaining momentum in the realm of design.

In 2008, Charlotte Rivers published one the few books currently written on the style of maximalism. "Ornament is no longer a crime," she proclaimed. "Architecture is more curvaceous, fashion more glamorous, design more decorative. Silhouette and botanical motifs are taking over from rigorous, simple lines and muted tones. A profusion of color and luxury, brimming with excess, is stating the case for a return to sensuality."[180]

Focusing on graphic design, Rivers explored maximal themes from the viewpoint of decoration, sensuality, luxury, and fantasy, highlighting such designers as Kam Tang and Andrew Wyatt, as well as a wealth of design firms based in the United States, Europe, and Japan such as Surface to Air and Vault 49. The intricate editorial work of UK-based Kam Tang, for example, has appeared in a variety of publications from The Guardian to Wallpaper magazine and has more recently contributed to the brand identity of London's Design Museum. Commissioned by the Graphic Thought Facility to create a series of illustrations for the Royal College of Art's annual prospectus (his alma mater), Tang produced a highly detailed surrealistic, Pop-meets-Escher line drawing of the academy, complete with ice-cream truck parked outside. The illustration is whimsically unsettling in its Japanese anime-esque sense of visual overload. Yet, it was meant to represent the Royal Academy of Art experience. The Royal Academy of Art is not the only institution to seek revitalization through a less-than-traditional approach to visual style. More and more, designers are turning to maximalist principles for branding, advertising, and package design. They import freely from past and present, like Swedish designer Hanna Werning, whose wallpaper and stationary designs echo the design aesthetic of nineteenth-century maximalist William Morris.[181]

But the fascination with maximalist approaches has by no means been limited to the two-dimensional realm. Gaining strong momentum in recent years is maximalist interior design. Noted designers Mario Buatta, Kelly Wearstler, and Miles Redd each embrace the maximalist spirit in varying degrees. Indeed Wearslter's approach to design could be used to describe maximalist painters, such as Leighton-Lundberg or Takashi Murakami: "There is a joy in designing a space without limitations and restrictions, where excess is encouraged and unlikely pairings create beautiful and

---

[178] Bonnie Wertheim, "The Maximalists Are Coming." *The New York Times*, October 4, 2017. https://www.nytimes.com/2017/10/04/fashion/ugly-design-decor-hardcore.html

[179] Janelle Zara, "Why is Maximalism taking over the world?" *The Architect's Newspaper*, June 21, 2017. https://archpaper.com/2017/06/maximalism-design-movement/#gallery-0-slide-0

[180] Charlotte Rivers, *Maximalism: The Graphic Design of Decadence & Excess* (Crans-Près-Céligny; Hove: RotoVision, 2008), 8.

[181] Additional examples include the husband and wife team Anna and Nathan Bon of Rifle Paper Co. and Sara Harding of Robert and Stella.

unexpected harmonies."[182] When the traditional, mass-marketed Country Living published, "20 Vibrant Rooms that Prove Minimalism Is Out, Maximalism Is In" in early 2017, it was official: maximalism had reached the mainstream:

> Does pared-down décor read "plain" and "sterile" to you? Have friends and family ever mocked you for what they dubbed your "overdone" décor and knack for collecting eclectic knick-knacks? Get ready to say "I told you so" because the days of modern minimalism may be nearing an end. Taking its place? Maximalism. Think vibrant hues and wild wallpaper prints instead of white and gray shades, layered rugs cozying up bare floors, tons of texture, and luxe touches of gold. Maximalists courageously douse their homes in color and patterns, preferring warm, inviting nooks over the stark spaces that you've probably already seen all over Pinterest.[183]

Interior design a-listers and mass-marketed media aside, maximalism is becoming more aggressive, extreme, and experimental. Maximalist design does not simply denote a reaction to minimalism, however subtle or understated. The new maximalists are bold, assertive, and intense. Their works can be found not only in functional interiors, but also in department stores, galleries, and museum spaces. For example, the shared Brooklyn studio of rising stars Misha Kahn and Katie Stout has been described as, "A kind of clubhouse for outlandish furniture something of a Willy Wonka wonderland."[184] Veteran artists Maurizio Cattelan and Pierpaolo Ferrari ventured into similar twisted and whimsical territory for the 2017 exhibition, "Toiletpaper Paradise," in partnership with Cadillac House. Flooring and wallpaper covered in large format images of spaghetti and tomato sauce unified this multi-room psychedelic installation of furniture and almost-believable interior decorations. "Toiletpaper Paradise" linked maximalist approaches from across the arts to form a three-dimensional amalgamation of assemblage, interior design, and contemporary genre with an undeniable dose of humor, irony, and ludicrousness. While maximalism is a highly visual style, its impact is not exclusively retinal. Much more than a reaction to minimalist sterility, maximalist art and design reflects underlying social and cultural shifts that relate to more than aesthetics alone.

MAXIMALISM & CONTEMPORARY CULTURE

As the history of art can attest, maximal approaches are by no means novel. From Greek Geometric pottery to Gothic architecture, baroque sculpture, Rococo

---

[182] Lindsey Mather, "Top Designers Debate Minimalism vs. Maximalism." *Architectural Digest*. August 5, 2016. https://www.architecturaldigest.com/story/designers-debate-maximalist-minimalist-homes

[183] Taysha Murtaugh, "20 Vibant Rooms That Prove Minimalism Is Out, Maximalism Is In." *Country Living*, January 31, 2017. http://www.countryliving.com/home-design/decorating-ideas/g4057/maximalist-interior-design-ideas/

[184] Katie Herriman, "The Playful Cartoonish Designs of a Furniture Wunderkind." *The New York Times Style Magazine*. Feb. 22, 2016. https://www.nytimes.com/2016/02/22/t-magazine/art/furniture-designer-misha-kahn-friedman-benda.html

ornamentation and Victorian design, artists have celebrated the freedom, frivolity, and luxury of visual abundance. But, just as pendulum swings between different artistic polarities (like *colorito* vs. *disegno* or expressionism vs. intellectuality), one might ask the question—what is it about visual overload that fascinates artists and connects with viewers? Is it just visual pleasure that motivates the maximal approach, or is there a more deeply rooted stimulus? To seek answers for these questions, the authors will narrow the scope of investigation to two themes recurrent in the work of Jeanne Leighton-Lundberg: gender and genre scenes.

Although maximalism can be registered on a broad spectrum, the theme of gender is recurrent in the works of many artists, often with regard to questioning or addressing stereotypes. Such is the case with contemporary portraitist Kehinde Wiley, the artist selected to paint the official portrait of former U.S. president Barack Obama for the Smithsonian National Portrait Gallery in Washington D.C. In many ways, the work of Leighton-Lundberg, a conservative painter of white women in domestic settings, seems like the ideological antithesis of the New York City-based Wiley, known for his portraits of black sitters in heroic poses. Yet, both artists share a common core of maximalism, art historical references, and the exploration of gender identity. Just as Leighton-Lundberg appropriated from the art historical past to create the recognizable women of her "Favorite Ladies" series, Wiley has appropriated from highly recognizable old master paintings to create his "The World Stage" series, which questions the social coding of race and gender. For example, his celebrated *Napoleon Leading the Army Over the Alps* (2005), features a young black man dressed in camouflage and assuming the iconic pose Jacques-Louis David's *Bonaparte Crossing the Alps* (1801). The ornate red and gold background calls to mind the intricate patterns of luxurious French tapestries, while at the same time creating a stylistic disjunction—a handsome, young black man in the trappings of European culture. Wiley uses pattern, decoration, and appropriation very carefully in order to make specific statements on gender and race:

> [The artwork] asks, 'What are these guys doing?' They're assuming the poses of colonial masters, the former bosses of the Old World. Whenever I do photo shoots for paintings, I pull out a stack of books, whether it be something from the High Renaissance or the late French Rococo or the 19th century, it's all thrown together in one big jumble. I take the figure out of its original environment and place it in something completely made up. Most of the backgrounds I end up using are sheer decorative devices. Things that come from things like wallpaper or the architectural façade ornamentation of a building, and in a way, it robs the painting of any sense of place or location, and it's located strictly in an area of the decorative. For the backgrounds in the World Stage Series, I look for traditional decorative objects, textiles, or devotional objects of that culture to draw upon.[185]

---

[185] "About," Kihinde Wiley, accessed December 30, 2017. http://kehindewiley.com/

Locating his works in "area[s] of the decorative," Wiley uses maximal techniques to create coded statements on race, masculinity, celebrity, and luxury that span European aristocracy to New York hip-hop culture. Much like Leighton-Lundberg, Wiley relies heavily on appropriation from European cultural history to draw complex connections and to form layered visual narratives. "By superimposing the opulent worlds of rulers and rappers," art historian Krista Thompson noted, "Wiley sought to visualize conventions for representing power in European portraiture on the surface of his paintings.[186]

In addition to appropriating art historical content in maximalist fashion, Wiley and Leighton-Lundberg share many commonalities through their similar maximalist approaches. Leighton-Lundberg's works ask questions about the visualization, power, and identity of women; Wiley does precisely the same, although with African American male subjects. Both elevate underrepresented voices: Leighton-Lundberg mused about what the "Favorite Ladies" would say if they could speak; Wiley considers "the consumption and production of blackness [a]nd how blackness is marketed to the world."[187] Both artists use surface decoration, vivid color, and visual overload to convey social messages. As noted above, Leighton-Lundberg elevated the concept of the female community. Her dinner parties are meetings points for women of different centuries and cultures; places where women can talk freely of their lives, their experiences, and their struggles. She understood that women's lives take many forms and visualized this collective female experience in vibrant, maximalist form. Wiley likewise focuses on expressing shared identity with relationship to gender symbolism, even exploring themes related to commodity and capitalism. Krista Thompson asks: "Given that historically surfacist ways of seeing have been related to the market economy and the visual production of commodities, what might hip-hop's surface aesthetics, as represented by Wiley, reveal about the commodity status of blackness historically and in late capitalism? Is bling a contemporary reappearance of the shine of blackness as commodity in the global marketplace?"[188]

Cleary, the works of Wiley and Leighton-Lundberg could be distinguished on many levels; the authors do not intend to oversimplify the messages or philosophies of these artists by emphasizing only cosmetic connections. However, the authors believe it is highly significant that Wiley and Leighton-Lundberg selected a maximalist approach to communicate particular themes and ideologies that would connect strongly with their audiences. This parallel relates to the fundamental nature of maximalism as an expressive departure from academism and traditionalism, a form of visual overload and artistic rebellion well suited to expressing themes related to personal identity and cultural history. The appropriative tendencies of maximalism nourish these themes, particularly the reliance upon the history of art and design. In this connection, maximal artists are able to build endless conceptual layers from visual references, be it an elaborate baroque pattern that conjures thoughts of

---

[186] Krista Thompson, "The Sound of Light: Reflections on Art History in the Visual Culture of Hip-Hop." *The Art Bulletin* 91, no. 4 (2009): 490.
[187] Kehinde Wiley, quoted in Paul Young, "The Re-Masters," *Daily Variety Magazine*, June 2, 2006, 33.
[188] Thompson, 496.

aristocratic entitlement, or a banquet table hosting the nude and morally questionable Victorine Meurant, courtesy Manet's *Luncheon on the Grass*. Such coded references speak volumes. They provide a framework in which to question representation and cultural classifications. Returning to the theme of Part vs. Whole, appropriative visual references do not function merely as decorative flourishes in maximalist works. Far from it, the proliferation of individual components often comprises the heart and soul of the work by creating extensive layers of meaning for the viewer to unpack.

Another contemporary maximalist who understands this principle well is Mickalene Thomas, as discussed earlier. Fascinatingly, Thomas's artist's statement could double for Leighton-Lundberg's: "Thomas introduces a complex vision of what it means to be a woman and expands common definitions of beauty. Her work stems from her long study of art history and the classical genres of portraiture, landscape, and still life."[189] Thomas, who identifies Manet and Matisse as sources of inspiration, focuses on investigating "notions of beauty from a contemporary perspective infused with the more recent influences of popular culture and pop art."[190] Like Wiley, Thomas explores themes related to black celebrity, identity, and Blaxploitation. Although, more like Leighton-Lundberg, Thomas focuses on the female perspective, typically in portraits and images of women in domestic interiors, such as the painting, *This Girl Could be Dangerous* (2007), which depicts a seated African American woman, confidently posed and looking directly at the viewer from a room bedecked in an array of 1970s inspired patterns. Like Leighton-Lundberg, Thomas is highly influenced by personal memory, family, and childhood experiences. She explains that her interest in 1970s textiles has less to do with Blaxploitation than with memories from her youth, such as her grandmother's preference of reupholstering and patching up furniture, rather than buying new.[191]

Thomas also borrows heavily from European art history, recreating familiar scenes such as Manet's *Luncheon on the Grass* (1863), which is echoed in *Le Déjeuner sur l'herbe: Les trois femmes noires* (2010), which features three black women, rather than two men and two women, as in the original. This brightly hued, mural-sized work is composed of Thomas's signature blend of rhinestones, acrylic, and enamel on wood. It embraces the maximalist love of texture, assemblage, fractured shapes, and the push-and-pull between part and whole. Patterns abound in this contemporary picnic, which focuses strongly on the concepts of gender and beauty. In Thomas's words, "I think beauty is one of the most powerful elements but there's a positive and negative side to it, as there's a positive and negative side to most things in life. We respond to beauty, its seduction and attraction, yet what that has done culturally to people that are subject to universal codes of beauty has been devastating. Still beauty is something we aspire to and continue to be seduced by."[192]

---

[189] Mickalene Thomas, Mickalene Thomas, accessed December 30, 2017. http://mickalenethomas.com/bio.html
[190] Ibid.
[191] Maja Horn, "The Multiple Media and Modes of Visibility of Mickalene Thomas." *Art Pulse.* http://artpulsemagazine.com/the-multiple-media-and-modes-of-visibility-of-mickalene-thomas
[192] Mickalene Thomas and Sean Landers, "Mickalene Thomas." *BOMB,* no 116 (2011): 38. http://www.jstor.org/stable/23037796.

Thomas's assessment calls to mind Leighton-Lundberg's words, as previously quoted: "Everything has been so male oriented. 'Fashion,' for example, is such a masculine idea. I see women running around in these short skirts and long jackets and they can't even sit down. Why do they do that? They want to please."[193] Just as Leighton-Lundberg was grappling with the concepts of beauty and fashion in the last decades of the twentieth century, Thomas continues this dialogue in the twenty-first century with a renewed interest in maximalist contemporary genre.

THE LEGACY CONTINUES

Building upon historical styles, contemporary maximalist trends express the complexity of contemporary culture. By celebrating excess, decorative overload, and controlled chaos, Maximalism is highly suitable to communicating open-ended questions that require the viewer to explore layers of symbolic and visual content. Although highly visual, Maximalism is not a passive style; it demands attention from and interaction with the viewer. Yet, as apparent in the works of countless artists and designers, Maxmalism does not embrace sensory overload for the sake of sensory overload: the highly charged visual qualities of this approach invite the viewer to consider social/cultural themes related to such relevant topics as gender, identity, and consumer culture.

Yet, Maximalism is in many ways a conflicted style. Like contemporary culture itself, maximal approaches contain an embedded dichotomy: although often associated with rebelliousness, limitlessness, and experimentation, maximal approaches by definition embrace luxury, extravagance, and overindulgence—qualities deeply embedded in the elite art patronage system of the European past. While the "more is more" attitude can be interpreted as a reaction against ascetic minimalism, it also connotes work that is more time intensive, more costly to produce, and possibly, more expensive. Indeed, we often associate aesthetic overindulgence with the creators and consumers of such decadent styles as Baroque, Rococo, and Beaux Arts, as well as their many variants, right down to contemporary celebrity and billionaire culture of the Trump Era. Maximal approaches signify a return to the luxury commodity, the creation of objects of awe and visual wonder worthy of cabinets of curiosity. By appropriating from "elite" visual culture—be it "Favorite Ladies" imported from celebrated art historical canvases or the poses and costumes of European aristocrats, maximalists in many ways elevate the very culture they seek to rebel against. Although, perhaps this contradiction is precisely the point, for maximalism is anything but transparent.

---

[193] Ibid.

CHAPTER 6

Conclusion

The first artist to identify Maximalism as her formal stylistic approach, Jeanne Leighton-Lundberg's work is a synthesis of modernist and postmodernist influences channeled through a lens of pattern theory and symbolism. While exhibiting visual markers and themes aligned with Pattern & Decoration, Leighton-Lundberg's signature style arose independent from the underpublicized movement—an artistic form of convergent evolution, as she and artists such as Joyce Kozloff, unbeknownst to each other, responded to Minimalism and Conceptualism in similar ways. It is at the juncture of P&D and Maximalism that Leighton-Lundberg's color-drenched canvases lie; filled with geometric and floral patterns, each of her defining series represent a portion of her legacy.

An analysis of her still lifes reveals her interest in fauvist-like color, multisensory qualities, and kinetic influences, as well as the emphasis she placed on structure through the use of clearly defined shapes and patterns within flattened planes which ignore the perspective rules of illusionism. The "Reclining Figures" are more self-reflexive, exploring the Feminine, matriarchy, ideal womanhood, and even the theme of nourishment, in a manner which can at once be viewed as a challenge to the iconic imagery of female nudes throughout art history. Her "Family Life" series is explicitly an exploration of pattern theory, which Leighton-Lundberg used to convey coded messages about time, relationships, life, and religion in a manner that melds genre painting and cubist tendencies in a way that only Maximalism can explain. Lastly, the iconic "Favorite Ladies" series incorporates blatant appropriation and feminist theory to reveal the influence of specific artists' work on her Maximalist thesis while simultaneously questioning their figurative and literal treatment of subjects. While certain themes are more obvious in one series over another, with few exceptions each of these visual assertions is present in every series. This can be explained in part by Leighton-Lundberg's methodology and the fact that her various series were not created completely consecutively. When placed chronologically, the concurrent nature of her work reveals the way that she explored Maximalism organically, allowing her work on one painting to influence the creation of others and in some cases even the complete overhaul of colorwork in previously "completed" works.

Leighton-Lundberg's pioneering Maximalist methodology is historically significant as the fulcrum between the avant-garde P&D artists of the 1970s and the recent upsurge in maximalist methods employed in art and design by contemporary artists. Maximalism has grown from a feminist response to Minimalism which explored non-Western approaches to art, new uses for domestic materials, color, pattern, and symbolism, to today's Maximalism—an almost indefinable, no-holds-barred, all-encompassing, anything-and-everything movement. How would Leighton-Lundberg respond to the impressive growth of Maximalism from reactionary art to a movement so widespread it may one day describe the Zeitgeist of the 21st century? It is impossible to say. But there is no doubt she would respond to its proliferation as passionately as she did to its inception.

BIBLIOGRAPHY

"About." *Kehinde Wiley*. Accessed December 30, 2017. http://kehindewiley.com/.

Aleci, Linda S. "In a Pig's Eye: The Offence of Some Living American Women Artists." *Mary Beth Edelson*. Accessed June 8, 2015. http://www.marybethedelson.com/essay_pigeye.htm.

Bradley-Evans, Martha Sonntag. "Women in the Arts: Evolving Roles and Diverse Expressions." In *Women in Utah History: Paradigm or Paradox?* Eds. Scott Patricia Lyn, Thatcher Linda, and Whetstone Susan Allred (Logan, Utah: Utah State University Press, 2005): 324-59.

Brooklyn Museum, "Exhibitions: Fred Tomaselli," accessed June 8, 2015, http://www.brooklyn museum.org/exhibitions/fred_tomaselli/.

Broude, Norma. "The Pattern and Decoration Movement." *The Power of Feminist Art.* Eds. Norma Broude, Mary D, Gerrard, Judith K. Brodsky. New York: Abrams, 1996.

———. "Review of "Dealing with Degas: Representations of Women and the Politics of Vision" by Richard Kendall and Griselda Pollock." *Women's Art Journal.* Vol. 16, No. 2.

Broude, Norma and Mary D. Garrard, "Feminist Art History and the Academy: Where Are We Now?" *Women's Studies Quarterly.* Vol 25, No. 1/2 (1997), 214.

Broude, Norma, Mary D. Garrard, and Judith K. Brodsky. *The Power of Feminist Art: The American Movement of the 1970s, History and Impact.* New York: H.N. Abrams, 1994: 16.

Chevreul, M.E. *The Principle of Harmony and Contrast of Colors.* Trans. Charles Martel. London: Longman, Brown, Green, and Longmans, 1855. https://archive.org/stream/principles harmo00martgoog#page/n6/mode/2up.

Chisholm, Madeline. "Women, Marriage, Education, and Occupation in the United States from 1940-2000." *U.S. History Through Census Data.* Dartmouth College. Last modified November 2016. https://journeys.dartmouth.edu/censushistory/2016/11/03/women-marriage-and-education-in-the-united-states-from-1940-2000/.uly 1, 2018,

Clark, Carol Lea. "Jeanne Leighton-Lundberg," *Southwest Art Magazine*, October 1989: 87.

"Clarke, Jeanne Leighton-Lundberg (1925)." *Springville Museum of Art.* Accessed August 5, 2016. http://www.smofa.org/collections/browse.html?x=artist&artist_id=431.

Clarke, Jeanne Leighton-Lundberg. "Inheritance I." Artist Statement, 1991.

———. "A Considered Proposition of Reality: The Maximum Statement." Master's thesis, Brigham Young University, 1980.

———. "Reflections on the Garden of Eden: A Testimony in Color A Personal Biography of Jeanne Leighton-Lundberg Clarke Our Pioneer by Her Son." Unpublished manuscript, 2016.

Clarke, Matthew. Interview by Rebekah Monahan. November 9, 2013.

———. Jeanne Leighton-Lundberg Clarke funeral service, Provo, Utah, March 1, 2014.

Clendenen, Alvis. "Experiencing Hildegard: Jungian Perspectives." Wilmette, Ill.: Chiron Publications, 2009.

Cochrane, Kira. "Women in art: why are all the 'great' artists men?" *The Guardian.* May 24, 2013. Accessed March 15, 2015. https://www.theguardian.com/lifeandstyle/the-womens-blog-with-jane-martinson/2013/may/24/women-art-great-artists-men.

Colpitt, Frances. "The Shape of Painting in the 1960s." *Art Journal* 50, no. 1 (1991): 52-56.

Cotter, Holland. "Scaling a Minimalist Wall with Bright, Shiny Colors." *New York Times.* January 15, 2008, http://www.nytimes.com/2008/01/15/arts/design/15patt.htm.

Crimp, Douglas. "The End of Painting." *October* 16 (1981): 69-86.

"Cubism." *Guggenheim Collection Online*, Solomon R. Guggenheim Foundation, Accessed December 30, 2017, www.guggenheim.org/artwork/movement/cubism.

DelPlato, Joan. "Multiple Wives, Multiple Pleasures: Representing the Harem, 1800-1875." *Fairleigh Dickenson University Press.* 2002: 9.

"Edouard Manet Luncheon on the Grass." *Musée D'Orsay: Works in Focus.* 2006. Musée D'Orsay. Accessed August 1, 2014.
    http://www.museeorsay.fr/index.php?id=851&L=1&tx_commentaire_pi1[showUid]=7123.
Ercolino, Stefano. *The Maximalist Novel: From Thomas Pynchon's Gravity's Rainbow to Roberto Bolano's 2666.* New York: Bloomsbury Academic, 2015.
"Exhibitions: The Dinner Party by Judy Chicago." *Brooklyn Museum.* Accessed June 8, 2015,
    http://www.brooklynmuseum.org/exhibitions/dinner_party/.
Flores, Tatiana and Florida State University Museum of Fine Arts. "More is More: Maximalist Tendencies in Recent American Painting." Tallahassee, Fla: Florida State University, Museum of Fine Arts, College of Visual Arts, Theatre and Dance, 2007. http://mofa.cvatd.fsu.edu/resources/archive/pages/learning/resources/moreismore.pdf.
"Frank Stella." *Guggenheim Collection Online.* Accessed December 12, 2017.
    https://www.guggenheim.org/artwork/artist/frank-stella.
Gao, Minglu. *Total Modernity and the Avant-Garde in Twentieth-Century Chinese Art.* Cambridge: MIT Press, 2011.
"Get the Facts." *National Museum of Women in the Arts.* Accessed June 8, 2015, http://nmwa.org/advocate/get-facts#sthash.w1H94Ruq.dpuf.
Gray, Sharon. "Interview with Rebekah Monahan." June 20, 2014.
Herriman, Katie. "The Playful Cartoonish Designs of a Furniture Wunderkind." *The New York Times Style Magazine.* Feb. 22, 2016. https://www.nytimes.com/2016/02/22/t-magazine/art/furniture-designer-misha-kahn-friedman-benda.html.
Herwitz, Daniel. *Making Theory/Constructing Art: On the Authority of the Avant-Garde.* Chicago: University of Chicago Press, 1996.
Hofmann, Hans, Sara T. Weeks and Barlett H. Hayes, eds. *The Search for the Real and Other Essays.* Cambridge, MA: MIT Press, 1967.
Horn, Maja Horn. "The Multiple Media and Modes of Visibility of Mickalene Thomas." *Art Pulse.* Accesed December 29, 2017. http://artpulsemagazine.com/the-multiple-media-and-modes-of-visibility-of-mickalene-thomas.
Johns, Elizabeth. *American Genre Painting: The Politics of Everyday Life.* New Haven: Yale University Press, 1993.
Joyce, Wendy Nolan. "Sculpting the Modern Muse: Auguste Clésinger's "Femme Piquée Par Un Serpent."" *Nineteenth-Century French Studies, Col.* 35, no. 1 (2006): 166-88. http://www.jstor.org/stable/23538385.
Kandinsky, Vasily. *On the Spiritual in Art.* Ed. and trans. Hilla Rebay. New York: Solomon R. Guggenheim Foundation. https://openlibrary.org/books/OL24645958M/On_the_spiritual_in_art.
Katz, Wendy Jean. *Regionalism and Reform: Art and Class Formation in Antebellum Cincinnati.* Columbus: Ohio State University Press, 2002.
Kelly, R.R. "Recollections of Josef Albers," *Design Issues* 16, no. 2 (2000): 3-24.
Kiilerich, Bente. "Savedoff, Frames, and Parergonality." *The Journal of Aesthetics and Art Criticism* 59, no. 3 (2001): 320-23. http://www.jstor.org/stable/432331.
Knakkergaard, Martin. Review of *Frank Zappa, Captain Beefheart and the Secret History of Maximalism,* by Michel Delville; Andrew Norris, *Popular Music* 27, No. 2 *(May 2008)*: 328-29. Stable URL: http://www.jstor.org/stable/40212389.
Landi, Ann. "Dancing with Degas." *ARTNEWS.* March 1, 2010. Accessed December 2014. http://www.artnews.com/2010/03/01/dancing-with-degas/.
Lasky, Julie. "Maximalism: The Lush New Décor Look That's Vanquishing Minimalism." *The Wall Street Journal.* January 26, 2017. https://www.wsj.com/articles/the-lush-new-decor-look-thats-vanquishing-minimalism-1485463384.
Leighton-Lundberg, Jeanne. "Inheritance 1." Artist Statement. Unpublished. Fall 1991.
———. "Loving Challenge" *American Mothers Inc. Publication.* c. 1990-1998.

———. "Statement of Purpose." Artist Statement. Unpublished. c. 1990-1992.

———. "Symbolist." Artist Statement. Unpublished. c. 1990-1992.

Lichfield, John. "The Moving of the Mona Lisa." *The Independent.* February 2, 2005. Accessed June 15, 2015. http://www.independent.co.uk/news/world/europe/the-moving-of-the-mona-lisa-6149165.htm.

Lubin, David M. *Picturing a Nation: Art and Social Change in Nineteenth-century America.* New Haven: Yale University Press, 1994.

"Maximalism." *SensAgent.* Accessed June 8, 2015, http://dictionary.sensagent.com/Maximalism/en-en/.

Mather, Lindsey. "Top Designers Debate Minimalism vs. Maximalism." *Architectural Digest.* August 5, 2016. https://www.architecturaldigest.com/story/designers-debate-maximalist-minimalist-homes.

Murakami, Takashi. "Why More Is More." *Esquire.* August 17, 2008. http://www.esquire.com/style/a4917/takashi-murakami-0908/.

Murray, Derek Conrad. "Mickalene Thomas: Afro-Kitsch and the Queering of Blackness." *American Art* 28, no. 1 (2014): 9-15. doi:10.1086/676624.

Murtaugh, Taysha. "20 Vibant Rooms That Prove Minimalism Is Out, Maximalism Is In." *Country Living.* January 31, 2017. http://www.countryliving.com/home-design/decorating-ideas/g4057/maximalist-interior-design-ideas/.

Nochlin, Linda. "Starting from Scratch: The Beginnings of Feminist Art History," in *The Power of Feminist Art: The American Movement of the 1970s, History and Impact, eds.* Norma Broude and Mary D. Garrard. New York: H.N. Abrams, 1994.

O'Leary, Elizabeth L. Lilly Martin Spencer's Peeling Onions, ca. 1852." *Seeing America: Paintings and Sculpture from the Collection of the Memorial Art Gallery.* Memorial Art Gallery, University of Rochester. 2006. Accessed June 19, 2018, https://mag.rochester.edu/seeingAmerica/pdfs/10.pdf

"Pablo Picasso's love affair with women." *The Telegraph.* February 13, 2009. Accessed October 15, 2016. http://www.telegraph.co.uk/culture/art/4610752/Pablo-Picassos-love-affair-with-women.htm.

Perreault, John. "Deluxe Redux: Legacies of the Pattern and Decoration Movement." *Pattern and Decoration: An Ideal Vision in American Art, 1975-1985.* Ed. Anne Swartz. Yonkers, NY: Hudson River Museum, 2007. https://books.google.com/books?id=VVIVs1GBGHIC&pg=PA7&source=gbs_toc_r&cad=4#v=onepage&q&f=false.

Perrone, Jeff. "Approaching the Decorative," *Artforum* XV (1976): 26-30.

———. "JOYCE KOZLOFF," *Artforum* XVIII (1979): 78-79.

"Picasso: Challenging the Past." *National Gallery of Art.* Accessed June 8, 2015. http://www.nationalgallery.org.uk/whats-on/past/picasso-challenging-the-past.

Pincus-Witten, Robert. *Postminimalism into Maximalism: American Art, 1966-1986.* UMI Research Press, 1987.

"Regalia." *Oxford Art Online.* Accessed April 25, 2015, http://www.oxfordartonline.com/subscriber/article/grove/art/T071111#T071115.

"Regulating Cosmetics, Devices, and Veterinary Medicine After 1938." Accessed February 13, 2015. http://www.fda.gov/AboutFDA/WhatWeDo/History/Origin/ucm055137.html.

"Reinterpreted Artworks: Le Déjeuner sur l'Herbe by Edouard Manet." *New Britain Museum of American Art.* April 27, 2010. Accessed March 4, 2015. https://nbmaa.wordpress.com/2010/04/27/reinterpreted-artworks-le-dejeuner-sur-l%E2%80%99herbe-by-edouard-manet/.

Richardson, John. "Degas and the Dancers." *Vanity Fair.* October 2002. Accessed October 15, 2016. http://www.vanityfair.com/news/2002/10/degas200210.

Riemer, Kristin E.M. Chinese Maximalism debuts. *UB Reporter*, October 9, 2003. http://www.buffalo.edu/ubreporter/archive/vol35/vol35n7/articles/Chinese Maximalism.html.

Rivers, Charlotte Rivers. *Maximalism: The Graphic Design of Decadence & Excess*. Crans-Près-Céligny; Hove: RotoVision, 2008.
Rodríguez, Ninón. "Cubism: A New Vision," Miami Dade College, n.d. Web. 20 Dec. 2017. https://www.mdc.edu/wolfson/Academic/ArtsLetters/art_philosophy/Humanities/Cubism/cubism%20front2.html.
Saleh, Patricia. "A Feminist-Symbolist." *Fine Art Collector International* 2, no. 2 (1992).
Schenkel, Ruth, "Edgar Degas (1834-1917): Painting and Drawing." *The Met's Heilbrunn Timeline of Art History*. The Metropolitan Museum of Art. October 2004. Accessed October 15, 2016. https://www.metmuseum.org/toah/hd/dgsp/hd_dgsp.html.
Shehan, Constance L., Mary Ann Burg, and Cynthia A. Rexroat, "Depression and the Social Dimensions of the Full-Time Housewife Role," *The Sociological Quarterly, Vol. 27 No. 3* (1986): 403-21.
Snyder, Thomas D., editor. "120 Years of American Education: A Statistical Portrait." Center for Educational Statistics, U.S. Department of Education, 1993. Accessed July 2018. https://nces.ed.gov/pubs93/93442.pdf
Springville Museum of Art. "Clarke, Jeanne Leighton-Lundberg." Accessed on June 8, 2015, http://www.springvilleartmuseum.org/collections/browse.html?x=artist&artist_id=431.
Thomas, Mickalene. *Mickalene Thoamas. Accessed December 30, 2017.* http://mickalenethomas.com/bio.html.
Thomas, Mickalene and Sean Landers. "Mickalene Thomas." *BOMB*, no 116 (2011): 30-38. http://www.jstor.org/stable/23037796
Thompson, Krista. "The Sound of Light: Reflections on Art History in the Visual Culture of Hip-Hop." *The Art Bulletin* 91, no. 4 (2009): 481-505.
Trachtman, Paul. "Degas and His Dancers." *Smithsonian Magazine*. April 2003. Accessed November 4, 2016. https://www.smithsonianmag.com/arts-culture/degas-and-his-dancers-79455990/.
Venning, Annabel. "How Picasso who called all women goddesses or doormats drove his lovers to despair and suicide." *Dailymail*. March 7, 2013, Accessed October 20, 2016. http://www.dailymail.co.uk/femail/article-2111329/How-Picasso-called-women-goddesses-doormats-drove-lovers-despair-suicide-cruelty-betrayal.html#ixzz37aIPowEA.
Walker, Kara. "Mickalene Thomas." *BOMB Magazine*, April 1, 2009. https://bombmagazine.org/articles/mickalene-thomas/.
Weinberg, H. Barbara, and Carrie Rebora Barratt. "American Scenes of Everyday Life, 1840–1910." *Heilbrunn Timeline of Art History*, The Metropolitan Museum of Art. September 2009. Accessed June 15, 2018. http://www.metmuseum.org/toah/hd/scen/hd_scen.htm (September 2009)
Wertheim, Bonnie. "The Maximalists Are Coming." *The New York Times*. October 4, 2017. https://www.nytimes.com/2017/10/04/fashion/ugly-design-decor-hardcore.html.
White Cube. "Fred Tomaselli." Accessed June 8, 2015. http://whitecube.com/artists/fred_tomaselli/.
Young, Paul. "The Re-Masters." *Daily Variety Magazine* (2006): 33.
Zara, Janelle. "Why is Maximalism taking over the world?" *The Architect's Newspaper*. June 21, 2017. https://archpaper.com/2017/06/maximalism-design-movement/#gallery-0-slide-0.

www.ingramcontent.com/pod-product-compliance
Lightning Source LLC
Chambersburg PA
CBHW040522220526
45473CB00013B/2948